THE
ULTIMATE
UNAUTHORIZED
STAR WARS
TRILOGY
TRIVIA
CHALLENGE

THE ULTIMATE UNAUTHORIZED STAR WARS TRILOGY TRIVIA CHALLENGE

James Hatfield
and George "Doc" Burt

KENSINGTON BOOKS

http://www.kensingtonbooks.com

KENSINGTON BOOKS are published by

Kensington Publishing Corp.
850 Third Avenue
New York, NY 10022

ISBN 1-57566-185-3

First Printing: March, 1997
10 9 8 7 6 5 4 3 2 1

Printed in the United States of America

This book is dedicated to:

George Lucas,
for brilliantly reinventing the classic fairy tale
and thrilling not only our generation, but countless
generations to come.

Bryan and Carla Grayson, two old and dear friends who rode the rough waters with me. With their dauntless faith, loyalty and dedication they kept the boat (and me) from capsizing when the white squall almost drowned us. Hey, guys, we finally made it to dry land! And especially for my wife, Nancy, who put up with me correcting page proofs on Christmas Day.
—*J.H.*

My daughter, Tammera, who is as beautiful, strong-willed and as much a survivor as Princess Leia; and to the newest joy in my life—Travis, my only grandson, who has showed me the way to the fountain of youth: *always, always* stay young at heart! This book is for these two wonderful people, who live in a galaxy far, far away . . . Utah!
—*"Doc"*

And to Sue Harke,
who is more than a researcher and archivist extraordinaire.
She is our sounding board, promotions and publicity coordinator,
master organizer of events, and keeper of the thickest black book
of sources and connections in all of science-fiction fandom.
But more importantly, she is our friend.
Thanks, Sue!

CONTENTS

ACKNOWLEDGMENTS   ix

INTRODUCTION: A long time ago in a galaxy far, far away.
   . . .   xv

STAR POWER, PART I   1

FROM FARM BOY TO JEDI KNIGHT: Luke Skywalker   9

I, ROBOT   15

BEHIND-THE-SCENES Star Wars: A New Hope   25

THE NAME GAME Star Wars: A New Hope   41

STAR TECH   42

ALIEN FACES & PLACES, PART I   51

THE WAN AND OBI: Ben Kenobi   60

EWOK THIS WAY   64

REBEL RUMBLINGS & IMPERIAL TRANSMISSIONS Star Wars:
   A New Hope   68

THE NITPICKER'S GUIDE: Star Wars: A New Hope   80

STAR WARFARE   93

PRINCESS BY VIRTUE, REBEL BY CHOICE: Leia Organa   100

SMUGGLER'S BLUES: Han Solo   104

WANTED: Dead or Alive   107

SOLO'S SIDEKICK: Chewbacca   111

BEHIND-THE-SCENES The Empire Strikes Back   114

THE NAME GAME The Empire Strikes Back   125

REBELS WITH A CAUSE   127

ALIEN FACES & PLACES, PART II   135

LORD OF THE DARK SIDE   143

REBEL RUMBLINGS & IMPERIAL TRANSMISSIONS The Empire
    Strikes Back   146

THE NITPICKER'S GUIDE: The Empire Strikes Back   161

APPEARANCES CAN BE DECEIVING: Jedi Master Yoda   166

THE EVIL EMPIRE   168

MASTER OF THE DARK SIDE: Emperor Palpatine   173

GAMBLER'S LUCK: The Lowdown on Lando Calrissian   176

BEHIND-THE-SCENES Return of the Jedi   179

THE NAME GAME Return of the Jedi   195

STAR POWER, PART II   197

REBEL RUMBLINGS & IMPERIAL TRANSMISSIONS Return of
    the Jedi   204

THE NITPICKER'S GUIDE: Return of the Jedi   221

AUTHORS' AFTERWORD   230

ANSWER KEY   235

JEDI KNIGHTHOOD SCORING LEGEND   267

BIBLIOGRAPHY   271

ACKNOWLEDGMENTS

Countless dedicated individuals contributed to make this book a reality. Acknowledgments must begin, of course, with all those who created the films, including the Master Jedi himself, George Lucas. He and his talented cadre of actors, directors, producers, puppeteers, special effect wizards, and other production specialists created the wonder and awe of a faraway galaxy . . . one of the most popular movie trilogies in the history of motion pictures—a pop cultural phenomenon, too, which has survived (as of this writing) for twenty years. Without these talented and dedicated men and women, there would be no fans, there would be no trivia, and there certainly would not be *The Ultimate Unauthorized Star Wars Trilogy Trivia Challenge.* Please understand, although we found the final installment a little too sugar-coated (especially those damn furry and cuddly Ewoks), we consider the *Star Wars* trilogy—either in original format or special edition—the epitome of movie magic and story telling.

Tracy Bernstein, our long-suffering editor at Kensington, once again applied her considerable talents as editor of *The Ultimate Unauthorized Star Wars Trilogy Trivia Challenge.* As always, Tracy, it was sheer and absolute joy to work with you and the rest of those talented folks on Third Avenue in New York, especially Barbara Bennett, Amy Stecher, April Benavides, and Adam Levison.

Special thanks also needs to go to Marcia Amsterdam, our liberal, comrade-in-arms literary agent who is just as much a delight to talk politics with as publishing. Thanks, Marcia, for selling this one and being so much fun to visit with in the morning, especially when you're skewing the "Bill-bashers."

For their assistance, support, and generosity, the following individuals deserve a special note of thanks: Canadian Brant Podlowski (for writing some of the best ad copy we've ever seen on the Net), Susan and Mike Bradshaw (for practicing guerrilla warfare at the bookstores and for being our bowling partners), Cindy McKitrick (for coming up with the George Lucas article when we were short on behind-the-scenes source material and, of course, for being a great boss and lunch companion), Debbie Alsup (our greatest fan and worldwide promoter), Ed and Judith Echols (for all their continued support, love and friendship and shared excitement for our publishing endeavors), Tommy and Sue Isaac (for promoting the other books on the Internet and giving us a place to unwind in the central Texas countryside one weekend), Mr. FedEx David Arnold and his son Ryan, Bill Lardie, CEO of Anderson Merchandisers, sci-fi afficionado Kris Swim at B. Dalton in the Northwest Arkansas Mall, Debra Broide and Diane Van Beuren (for all the publicity), Peggy Morton with Borders bookstore in Dallas, Jack and Phyllis Bergstrom, cigar-smoking Mike Hills at Barnes & Noble in Fayetteville, Frances LeBlanc (dynamite *really* does come in small packages), Crossroads' Tim Walbert, Peggy Smith with Hastings in Fayetteville, Monica Miceli at Borders bookstore in Las Vegas, Florence and Morrie Soetaert, Mark Elwood at the *Village Vista* (thanks for the front page story and excellent company over coffee one summer morning), Valorie Jones at Waldenbooks in Fayetteville, Danielle Walther at B. Dalton deep south in Alabama (for not only pushing our books, but also for being a favorite e-mail pal at the wee hours of the morning), and Virgil Rose and Jeannie Clark at the Tulsa Woodland Hills Mall Waldenbooks. Our deepest thanks, though, goes to author Ruby Jean Jensen for shining the light into the darkness; and finally, last but certainly not least, *Subspace Chatter* and *Warp 10* online editor Ruben Macias (for assisting us with our research, promoting our previous books, announcing our book signings, and always being there for us when we only had to ask).

Special acknowledgments from "Doc": I am forever indebted to James "J.R." Creek, my nephew and young Jedi Knight-in-training; Don Havlick, one of Houston, Texas', finest attorneys and whose dedication and professional service to his clients is un-equaled; Aunt Lulu, Juanita and Joyce Bryant, and George; Charles Erick and Ruth Shipp, two friends who were there even when the storm clouds gathered and the vultures circled; and Theresa "T.C." Barbero, my number one critic extraordinaire.

In addition, all of the following *Star Wars* fans' dedication and assistance in one way or another made this book possible: David C. Fein, Ryan Silva, Tim Elliot, Joe Forester, Peter Poulakakos, Evan Reynolds, Alec Usticke, James Addams, Mike Beidler, Don Bies, Bill Brownell, Chip Cataldo, Raymond W. Charmega, Steven Downer, Keith Evans, Nicky Wilson, D.J. Stewart, Kristin Mil-stead, Brent Lynch, Vian Lawson, Rob Laurie, Dave A. Lartigue, David A. Koran, Ed Hill, David Halstead, Jason M. Fischer, Mark R. Leeper, Glenn Saunders, Matthew Mohs, Jason Collier, Steve Stelter, Julie Lim, George "Jake" Tringali, Jeanne Mangum, Peter Ferguson, Skip Shayotovich, Scott Streeter, Ming Wathne, Eric Sansoni, Rebecca Moesta Anderson, Craig Carey, Roger M. Wilcox, Nicole Nuke, Keven Lewis, Peter Leyshan, Noah Nelson, John Warren, Rusty Miller, Eric Schaetzlein, Aditya Sood, James L. Belcher, Joshua Booth, Jeff DiBartolmeo, Jeremy Kennedy, Matt Bradshaw, Daniel Goldman, Ryan Smith, Bill Warren, Robert Alan Danforth, Craig MacKinnon, Rajiv Udani, Ray Rho, Brandon Gillespie, Todd Chambers, Scott B. Casteel, Aaron Romanowsky, Andy Hofle, Bryan Carolan Dunne, Cleavy McKnight, Dan Uslan, Daniel S. Highlands, Darryll Hobson, David Kember, Dax Shifrel, Doug Brod, Doug Tooley, Ed Hirsh, Jefferey Gold, John Hager-man, Mark Swartz, Michael Clark, Michael Palencar, Murray Chapman, Kevin Cox, Dan Wallace, Andrew Fustini, Donna Parker, Jack Skellington, Jim Fisher, Allen Newman, Erich Hurst, David Lebel and Harry Knowles. May the Force be with you all . . . always!

All the others who helped in some way to produce *The Ultimate Unauthorized Star Wars Trilogy Trivia Challenge* have our heartfelt thanks, and if we omitted your name, please forgive us. It certainly was not intentional.

"Nobody except Disney makes movies for young people anymore. I want to open up the whole realm of space for them."

—George Lucas in a 1977 interview

"It's sheer joy making things that don't exist."

—John Dykstra, *Star Wars* F/X wizard

"George [Lucas] said he would like for us to put together a creature shop. Some of the story points weren't clarified, but I have a feeling George works through telepathy."

—Phil Tippett, *Return of the Jedi* F/X

"Star Wars is a fairy tale, a fantasy, a legend . . . [that] taps the pulp fantasies buried in our memories, and because it's done so brilliantly, it reactivates old thrills, fears and exhilarations . . ."

—Film critic Roger Ebert

"I've always loved adventure films . . . I came to realize that since the demise of the western, there hasn't been much in the mythological fantasy genre available to the film audience. So instead of making 'isn't-it-terrible-what's-happening-to-mankind' movies, which is how I began, I decided that I'd try to fill that gap. I'd make a film so rooted in imagination that the grimness of everyday life would not follow the audience into the theater. In other words, for two hours, they could forget . . ."

—George Lucas

INTRODUCTION:
A Long Time Ago in a Galaxy Far, Far Away. . . .

Star Wars: A New Hope, The Empire Strikes Back and *Return of the Jedi,* with combined gross ticket sales of $1.3 billion worldwide, comprise the most successful trilogy in movie history with all three in the Top 15 box office hits of all time. At the end of 1995, 20th Century Fox rereleased a boxed set of the three modern classics to a new, global generation in thirty-eight countries. Millions of units were sold during the first week alone. And then in 1997, millions of fans got a chance to watch "special editions" of the trilogy when the films returned to theaters to celebrate the first movie's twentieth anniversary. Each film was restored, special effects enhanced, footage added, sound remastered, and in the process, a whole new generation of younger fans who had never seen the trilogy in theaters before were introduced to the ways of the Force.

The *Star Wars* trilogy is considered the largest entertainment franchise in the world (possibly the galaxy) with universal and timeless appeal across countries and demographic groups. The undisputed king of science-fiction marketing and media frenzy, the trilogy (like its intergalactic cousin *Star Trek*) has spawned best-selling reference books, comics, posters, action figures, interactive computer games, T-shirts, coffee mugs, calendars, Internet websites, online chat groups, fan organizations and conventions.

Star Wars, like *Star Trek,* is a universe filled with well-defined characters and situations and creatures and intergalactic politics. Conventions are held in cities all around the world throughout the year. Thousands of fans show up dressed as Luke Skywalker, Princess Leia, R2-D2, C-3PO, Darth Vader, Chewie, Obi-Wan Kenobi, Jawas, Ewoks, Imperial stormtroopers, or any number of *Star Wars'* myriad life-forms. And trivia contests are always a staple of every convention. Fan clubs abound by the hundreds around the globe, and in each issue of the organizations' magazines or newsletters there is always a trivia section. Thousands of *Star Wars* chat groups log on the Internet daily, devoting megabytes to critical reviews on such unique subjects as the *Millennium Falcon's* hyperdrive capabilities and "netpicking" the trilogy's plot oversights, production problems and technical screw-ups. *Star Wars* trivia generates some of the heaviest electronic traffic in cyberspace. Yet never has there been, in one volume, a collection of trivia questions and answers about the hugely popular *Star Wars* universe.

Until now.

In the spirit of any worthwhile trivia challenge of this magnitude and scope, there are a variety of different categories in this book. For example, the questions in the **STAR POWER** sections will adequately test your working knowledge of Rebel and Imperial spacecraft and surface vessels—from speeder bikes to TIE starfighters; **ALIEN FACES & PLACES** divisional categories will quiz participants on the trilogy's memorable alien creatures and their homeworlds. In addition, strategically placed throughout the book are trivia tests that address behind-the-scenes and on the sets of the movies, character dossiers (profiled by the Imperial Security Bureau and the Bothan Spy Network), and dialogue between the characters **(Rebel Rumblings & Imperial Transmissions).** Also included is a detailed listing of bloopers, scientific snafus, inconsistencies, impossibilities and just plain screw-ups from each installment of the trilogy. Testing methods are just as varied with a combination of multiple choice, fill in the blank, true or false, short answer, and matching.

All correct answers count as 1 point, except the specifically designed **JEDI MASTER BONUS** questions, which count as 5 points each because they are intended to seriously challenge the die-hard *Star Wars* fan.

In the back section of this book you will find the Answer Key, plus a specific line to calculate and enter your score as you play along per category. On the very last page you will compute your total score for this book's ultimate trivia challenge and determine your level of training success and status as a Jedi Knight.

You can start at the beginning with **STAR POWER** and work your way through this asteroid field of trivia questions, or flip around and pick out random questions that test your particular knowledge of **REBELS WITH A CAUSE** or behind-the-scenes of each of the movies or technical specifications in the **STAR TECH** section. However you want to approach this trivia challenge, you are sure to know more about the *Star Wars* universe when you've finished this book than you did when you started.

May the Force be with you!

James Hatfield & George "Doc" Burt

A Few Notes
about Source Material

One of the great ongoing debates in the *Star Wars* universe is the matter of what's canonical: what, in *Star Wars* terms, is "real," and which events never actually happened to Luke Skywalker, Han Solo, Princess Leia, Chewie, the droids, Darth Vader, the Emperor, or any of our beloved Rebel heroes or loathed Imperial villains?

Although the ongoing space saga has continued with a long line of hugely successful books in print, we have only used sources associated with the original trilogy (i.e. the movies themselves, the novelizations, the National Public Radio dramatizations, and reference sources such as West End Games' *Star Wars: The Movie Trilogy Sourcebook*, etc.). A comprehensive bibliography can be found in the final pages of this book.

Die-hard fans will immediately realize that there are a few nagging inconsistencies between the cinematic version of the trilogy and the best-selling novelizations (even though George Lucas penned the first book). Example: According to the *Star Wars: A New Hope* novel, Red Leader was the comm-unit designation for Rebel pilot Dutch's Y-wing during the Battle of Yavin. In the movie version, his designation was Gold Leader.

When in doubt, the general rule is to go with the trilogy's cinematic interpretation of the same events.

THE
ULTIMATE
UNAUTHORIZED
STAR WARS
TRILOGY
TRIVIA
CHALLENGE

STAR POWER
Part I

From the very first scene of Star Wars: A New Hope—*with the mammoth, wedge-shaped Star Destroyer and other smaller Imperial starfighters in pursuit of Princess Leia's Blockade Runner—to the climactic space battle to save the galaxy from the evil Empire in* Return of the Jedi, *the* Star Wars *trilogy is unrivaled for its cinematic depiction of awe-inspiring and powerful spacecraft and surface vehicles. To initiate your training as a Jedi Knight, you must first be challenged with a series of questions to adequately test your knowledge of Rebel and Imperial forces—from A-wing fighters to TIE interceptors, from speeder bikes to the colossal Death Star battle station. Remember the words of your mentor and Jedi Master Yoda, "Try not. Do or do not. There is no try."*

---

1. Which senior Imperial commanding officer claimed that the Death Star was the ultimate power in the universe?
   A. Admiral Ozzel
   B. Admiral Motti
   C. Admiral Griff

2. Identify the merchant ship on which Biggs Darklighter served as first mate, which was his first assignment after graduation from the Academy.

3. What custom-built feature made Darth Vader's TIE fighter different from other combat starfighters in the Imperial fleet?

A. It had angular solar-panel "wings"
B. It had triple ion engines
C. It was equipped with particle shielding

4. (Fill in the blank dialogue) Han Solo bragged to Luke Sky-walker and Ben Kenobi in the Mos Eisley cantina that the *Millennium Falcon* was the "ship that made the _____ run in twelve parsecs."

5. What was the fastest combat starfighter in either the Rebel Alliance or the Galactic Empire's fleet?
    A. A-wing
    B. TIE interceptor
    C. X-wing

6. How many Imperial Star Destroyers pursued the *Millennium Falcon* as it left Tatooine's Mos Eisley spaceport?
    A. One
    B. Two
    C. Three

JEDI MASTER BONUS #1

What Rebel Alliance combat fighter was built to go head-to-head with the Empire's TIE starfighter models?

---

7. (True or False) Five occupants was the seating capacity of a landspeeder.

8. How did the Rebel Alliance's General Dodonna describe the awesome firepower of the Death Star battle station?

9. Identify Admiral Ackbar's Mon Calamari-designed starship which served as his personal flagship during the decisive Battle of Endor.

A. *Adelphi Two*
B. *Repulse One*
C. *Home One*

10. In *The Empire Strikes Back,* how many Star Destroyers were shown in the Imperial fleet?
    A. Four
    B. Five
    C. Six

11. What repulsorlift airships were used to battle the AT-AT walkers on Hoth?

12. Who described the *Millennium Falcon* as the "fastest junk in the galaxy"?
    A. Han Solo
    B. Lando Calrissian
    C. Chewbacca

JEDI MASTER BONUS #2

Which vehicles or types of vehicles appear in both *Star Wars: A New Hope* and *The Empire Strikes Back*?

---

13. Which type of three-winged Imperial space shuttle resembled an inverted Y in flight?
    A. *Lambda*-class
    B. *Lancer*-class
    C. *Imperial*-class

14. (True or False) Even when a landspeeder was stationary it remained pendent about a meter off the surface terrain as an aftereffect of the engine-produced repulsor field.

15. Identify the Rebel star cruiser that was vaporized along with its entire crew by the second Death Star's primary weapon.

A. *Liberty*
B. *Intrepid*
C. *Victory*

16. What was the landing pad number on Bespin's Cloud City where the *Millennium Falcon* was docked on its visit to the mining colony after the Hoth battle?
    A. 273
    B. 327
    C. 732

17. What distinct characteristic gave the X-wing starfighter its name?

18. What type of immense, repulsorlift vehicle did Jabba the Hutt use as his personal transport for traveling across Tatooine's desert wastelands?

JEDI MASTER BONUS #3

What was the new landspeeder model on the galactic market that made Luke Skywalker's less valuable?

---

19. Which company designed and constructed the T-65 X-wing starfighter and the skyhopper T-16 airspeeder?
    A. THX Vehicles, Inc.
    B. DelphiWorks, Ltd.
    C. Incom Corporation

20. (Fill in the Blank) Pilots who flew the X-wings quite often referred to the small spacecraft as _____ fighters.

21. Which Imperial Star Destroyer intercepted and captured Princess Leia's Blockade Runner over Tatooine when she at-

tempted to smuggle the original Death Star's technical read-outs to the Rebel Alliance's High Command?

    A. *Executor*

    B. *Avenger*

    C. *Devastator*

22. What was the name of Darth Vader's personal flagship, which was a *Super*-class Star Destroyer?

23. How many starfighter squadrons were housed in the twenty hangar bays aboard Admiral Ackbar's *Home One* starship?

    A. 10

    B. 12

    C. 15

24. (Fill in the Blank) The old, multipurpose Corellian _____ had been nicknamed the Blockade Runner because pirates and smugglers repeatedly made use of its quick jump to hyperspace to avoid questions by Galactic authorities.

JEDI MASTER BONUS #4

What was another name for the *Home One*, the command ship from which Admiral Ackbar directed the Rebel fleet during the decisive Battle of Endor?

---

25. What was the Death Star's primary weapon?

26. The Rebel Alliance was able to exploit a vulnerability in the original Death Star's design which consequently led to its destruction. What was this massive weapon's weakness, at which fighter pilots aimed?

27. How many kilometers in diameter was the second, larger, Death Star?

   A. 140
   B. 160
   C. 180

28. What was another name for the four-legged Imperial trooper carrier and assault vehicle, AT-AT?

29. Besides "scout walker," what was the other nickname for the Imperial reconnaissance and defense vehicle, AT-ST?

30. Identify the Imperial Star Destroyer that was disabled temporarily during the Hoth battle by the Rebel Alliance's planet-based ion cannon.
   A. *Executor*
   B. *Avenger*
   C. *Devastator*

JEDI MASTER BONUS #5

How many meters long were the skiffs that Jabba the Hutt used as surface companion utility craft to his huge sail barge?

---

31. What was the name of bounty hunter Boba Fett's starfighter?

32. (Fill in the blank with the correct number) The small, one-person speeder bike was outfitted with _____ directional steering vanes.

33. (True or False) An *Imperial*-class Star Destroyer was 2.1 kilometers in length.

34. (True or False) In *Star Wars: A New Hope,* Han Solo and Chewie were able to find the Death Star by chasing a TIE fighter.

35. What vehicle did Luke Skywalker use on Tatooine in addition to his landspeeder?

36. In *Star Wars: A New Hope,* identify the modified force that immobilized the *Millennium Falcon* and compelled it to land on the Death Star.

JEDI MASTER BONUS #6

Which vehicles or types of vehicles appeared in *Star Wars: A New Hope,* but not in *The Empire Strikes Back?*

---

37. What was the shape of the conference room on the original Death Star?

38. (Fill in the Blank) The Rebel Alliance often converted _____ into transport ships as they did when they had to quickly evacuate the Hoth base.

39. Who owned the *Millennium Falcon* before Han Solo?

40. What course did the *Millennium Falcon* take when entering the asteroid belt in *The Empire Strikes Back?*
    A. 271
    B. 262
    C. 225.3

41. Where did the *Falcon* hide from the Imperial fleet after it emerged from the mouth of the colossal space slug?

42. What color were the atmospheric flying vehicles (patrol craft and traffic control cars) used outside of Bespin's Cloud City?
    A. White
    B. Gray
    C. Orange

JEDI MASTER BONUS #7

In *The Empire Strikes Back,* what vehicles and vessels (in addition to the *Millennium Falcon*) were seen in the Rebel ice hanger on Hoth?

FROM FARM BOY TO JEDI KNIGHT: LUKE SKYWALKER
Imperial Security Bureau (ISB) Dossier #487818

1. Luke believed that this moisture farmer on Tatooine was his natural uncle. What was his name?

2. In reality, who was the brother of Luke's guardian?

3. Identify Luke's foster mother, whom the boy called "aunt."

4. Who senselessly murdered the couple and why?

5. What was Luke's childhood nickname among the joyriding crowd from the nearby town of Anchorhead?
    A. Dreamer
    B. Wormie
    C. Lukie

6. Identify the power distribution facility located near Anchorhead that served as a meeting place for young Luke and his friends.
    A. Daed Industrial Plant
    B. Tosche Station
    C. Daquelon Depot

JEDI MASTER BONUS #1

Identify the insolent and arrogant mechanic at the Anchorhead power station who was also a boyhood friend of Luke.

---

7. What was the name of the mechanic's girlfriend?
    A. Carla
    B. Raylene
    C. Camie

8. (True or False) Wendy was another one of Luke's childhood friends who grew up with him on Tatooine.

9. Identify the future Rebel starfighter pilot whom Luke spent most of his teenage years with on Tatooine, racing landspeeders and skyhoppers, dreaming of galactic space battles and making plans to go to the Academy together.

10. What did Luke believe his father had done for a living before Ben Kenobi told him the truth?
    A. Served as a navigator on a space freighter
    B. Repaired water vaporators on Tatooine
    C. Piloted galactic "cruise" ships

11. (Fill in the Blank) Luke was surprised to learn that the crazy, elderly recluse whom he had always known as "_____Ben," was in actuality Obi-Wan Kenobi, a Jedi Knight.

12. What did Ben Kenobi give to Luke, which had once belonged to the boy's father?

JEDI MASTER BONUS #2

Why did Luke's "uncle" insist that he postpone his application to the Academy?

---

13. What was Luke playing with while C-3PO was taking his oil bath?
    A. Holomonsters
    B. His lightsaber
    C. A model ship

14. (True or False) Luke was left-handed.

15. (True or False) Ben Kenobi misled Luke by explaining that the boy's father, Anakin Skywalker, had been a trusted friend of Kenobi's, a comrade-in-arms during the Clone Wars, who was ultimately betrayed and murdered by Darth Vader.

16. Where did Luke obtain the rope that he and Princess Leia used to swing over the chasm in the Death Star battle station?

17. What did Luke ask Leia to hold just before they made their escape via the rope?

18. Luke's experience with racing his T-16 skyhopper through the treacherous Beggar's Canyon on Tatooine served him well when he was thrust into a key role as a Rebel starfighter pilot. What did he compare targeting the Death Star battle station's exhaust port to?

19. What military rank did Luke achieve after the Battle of Yavin?
    A. Captain
    B. Lieutenant
    C. Commander

20. What was Darth Vader's ultimate plan for Luke?

JEDI MASTER BONUS #3

Identify the regenerative chemical in which Luke was immersed to rapidly heal injuries sustained from an attack by a Wampa ice creature on Hoth.

---

21. How did Luke escape from the Wampa creature's ice cave lair?

22. Why did Luke remain outside on the frozen plains of Hoth when Han went back to Echo Base?

23. Who instructed Luke to travel to the swamp planet of Dagobah, where he was to find the Jedi Master Yoda and complete his training?

JEDI MASTER BONUS #4

Who referred to Luke as "the best bush pilot in the outer rim territories"?

---

24. (True or False) The front-line Rebel troops on Hoth witnessed Luke single-handedly bring down an Imperial troop transport and an assault craft AT-AT.

25. Who did Luke originally believe he encountered inside the dark, cavernous tree on Dagobah?

26. What did Luke "see" during his vision of the future when he became sensitive to the Force under Yoda's tutelage?

27. How did Luke ultimately escape from Darth Vader during their lightsaber battle on Cloud City?

JEDI MASTER BONUS #5

What three things did Luke lose during his first and tragic confrontation with Darth Vader in the bowels of Bespin's floating metropolis?

JEDI MASTER BONUS #6

Identify the piece of machinery Luke desperately clung to at the bottom of Cloud City.

---

28. What were Luke's first words after he was rescued by the *Millennium Falcon*?
    A. "Where's Han?"
    B. "Oh, Leia."
    C. "My presence here jeopardizes your lives."

29. What were the last words Luke said to Lando Calrissian and Chewbacca as they departed?
    A. "Take care, you two, and may the Force be with you."
    B. "Be careful, you two, and may the Force be with you always."
    C. "Don't worry, you two, with the help of the Force we'll rescue Han."

30. What color was the beam of the new lightsaber that Luke constructed?

31. Who smuggled Luke's lightsaber into Jabba the Hutt's desert palace on Tatooine?

32. (True or False) Luke took a blaster hit to his prosthetic hand that nearly incapacitated it during Han Solo's rescue and the destruction of the crime lord and his entire organization.

JEDI MASTER BONUS #7

Identify the manifestation of the Force that Luke used to verbally implant the suggestion of "you will take me to Jabba, now" into the mind of Bib Fortuna.

---

33. (Fill in the blank dialogue) Luke returned to Dagobah to complete his training as a Jedi Knight and to "keep a promise to an old _____."

34. What did a dying Yoda tell Luke was the only thing left to complete his training as a full Jedi?
     A. The ability to resist the dark side of the Force
     B. Accept the Force as a constant companion
     C. Confront Darth Vader a second time

35. Who warned Luke that he could not return his father to his own inner truth, to pull him back from the dark side?

36. Who informed Vader that Leia was Luke's twin sister, another Skywalker strong in the Force?

JEDI MASTER BONUS #8

(Fill in the blank dialogue)

When the Emperor failed in his efforts to corrupt Luke as he did his father, the evil leader of the Empire smiled down at the nearly unconscious young Jedi and once again assaulted him with another barrage of lightning bolts of energy from his fingers. "Young fool! Only now at the end, do you understand. Your _____ skills are no match for the power of the dark side."

JEDI MASTER BONUS #9

How old was Luke when he destroyed the original Death Star battle station?

I, ROBOT

In homage to the noted twentieth-century biochemist and prolific author, Dr. Isaac Asimov (1920–1992), who postulated robots would employ so-phisticated positronic computing devices in their brains, this section will test your knowledge of droids, the automatons of the Star Wars universe. Although most droids communicated via a program language of expressive beeps and whistles (R2-D2 is a classic example), we hope you spent enough time working with or around droids to pick up on their unique language and now have a comprehensive understanding of droid history and tech-nology.

---

1. What was the verbal command code function that instanta-neously overrode a droid's principal programming?
    A. Voice Annul: Alpha Omega Psi
    B. Audio Overturn: Delta 626
    C. Voice Override: Epsilon Actual

2. What type of droids specialized in the maintenance and repair of starships?

3. What was See-Threepio afraid would happen to him and Artoo-Detoo if Imperial forces captured them on the Blockade Runner?

4. What was another name for advanced surveillance and track-ing probots?

5. What three-word expression did C-3PO often articulate in semireligious context?
    A. "Thank the Creator!"
    B. "Thank the Maker!"
    C. "Thank the Builders!"

6. Identify the hulking, unwieldy-looking utility droids constructed and programmed for common labor assignments.
    A. Regis I Labor Droids
    B. Mark II Reactor Drones
    C. Benza XI Assembly Models

JEDI MASTER BONUS #1

In *Star Wars: A New Hope,* where did Luke Skywalker's uncle Owen tell his nephew he was planning to send R2-D2 and C-3PO and for what purpose?

---

7. (True or False) Pelvic servomotors rendered bipedal droids with the mechanism to effect movements in their legs.

8. Which series of popular astromech droids did Owen Lars initially procure from the Jawas before Luke Skywalker persuaded him to take the R2-D2 unit instead?
    A. R5 unit
    B. R6 unit
    C. R7 unit

9. What was another term used to describe a protocol droid?

10. Identify the type of medical droid that performed the operation to replace Luke Skywalker's severed hand with a prosthetic in *The Empire Strikes Back.*

    A. C-62 (See-Sixtoo)
    B. B-2B (B-Toobee)
    C. 2-1B (Too-Onebee)

11. How many limbs were constructed on a multipurpose tread-well robot?

12. What was another name for a droid's sound-producing vocabulator device, which permitted the automaton to speak in millions of languages?
    A. Vocoders
    B. Vocabs
    C. Vocal Regulators

JEDI MASTER BONUS #2

What type of droid was the battle-scarred bounty hunter IG-88?

---

13. Why didn't Imperial forces fire on R2-D2 and C-3PO's pod when they escaped from the Blockade Runner?

14. (True or False) Probots possessed the defensive ability to generate a protective force field.

15. (Fill in the blank dialogue) C-3PO bellowed, "Curse my _____ body" when he thought his friends were dying in the Death Star's immense trash compactor.

16. In *Star Wars: A New Hope*, what was the ever-fretting C-3PO afraid the Jawas were going to do with him and R2-D2?
    A. Disassemble them
    B. Sell them to the Empire, who would then transform them into slave droids
    C. Melt them down

17. Why did Luke Skywalker's uncle order him to take R2-D2 to Anchorhead?

18. (True or False) R5-D4 was the name designation of the droid that Luke and his uncle Owen first procured from the Jawa traders, which, when it showed signs of damage, was replaced by R2-D2.

JEDI MASTER BONUS #3

What were the three instructions Luke gave R2-D2 during the Battle of Yavin's assault on the first Death Star?

---

19. What was the name designation of EV-9D9's subordinate in Jabba the Hutt's Cyborg Operations, the department concerned with the torture of droids?
    A. 7D2
    B. 8D8
    C. 9D1

20. (True or False) BL-17s were primitive labor droids designed and constructed for the sole purpose of moving heavy objects from place to place.

21. (Fill in the Blank) When Luke Skywalker was cleaning R2-D2 and C-3PO for his uncle Owen, he found _____ scoring on the R2 unit.

22. (Fill in the blank dialogue) R2-D2 called C-3PO a "mindless _____ " when the larger droid refused to get into the escape pod in *Star Wars*.

23. Identify the diminutive, hand-held transmitting devices used to beckon droids by relaying signals to their restraining bolts.
    A. Callers
    B. Relayers
    C. Emitters

24. What language was C-3PO required to speak for Luke Sky-walker's uncle?
    A. Chodgen
    B. Bocce
    C. Lnach

JEDI MASTER BONUS #4

What type of engines provided the mobility for the Empire's interrogator droids?

---

25. (True or False) A human-droid relations specialist was a cyborg whose primary function was to provide an interface between humans and other droids.

26. Who gave C-3PO the nickname of "Goldenrod"?
    A. Han Solo
    B. R2-D2
    C. Lando Calrissian

27. Which antiquated droid units were still in service as medical assistants to the Rebel Alliance?
    A. MA-8
    B. SI-4
    C. FX-7

28. (True or False) Jabba the Hutt's sadistic Eve-Ninedenine droid was programmed with a deep, almost raspy male voice.

29. (Fill in the Blank) Droids could be automated to receive command control directions by way of a distinctive _____ pattern which usually belonged to the droid's master or immediate supervisor.

30. (Fill in the blank with the correct number) C-3PO was fluent in over _____ million galactic languages.

31. Name the captain of the Alderaanian consular ship *Tantive IV* whom C-3PO claimed he and R2-D2 belonged to until the ship was captured by the Empire.
    A. Antilles
    B. Shaddaa
    C. Byss

JEDI MASTER BONUS #5

Identify C-3PO's four types of receptors.

---

32. Which droid was considered an adept hologame player, often serving as an opponent for gangster Jabba the Hutt or one of his criminal associates at his palace on Tatooine?
    A. JH-487
    B. GB-486
    C. BG-J38

33. What small, cylinder-shaped apparatus kept a droid from straying away?

34. Unlike actual droids, these automatons possessed no aptitude for independent motivation and could only do what they were instructed to do. What were they?

35. (Fill in the Blank) An administrative assistant with artificial intelligence would be classified as a specially programmed _____ droid.

36. What was the actual name for a droid's mechanical "on and off" switch, or primary circuit breaker?

37. What was another name for a memory wipe, which was used to expunge all of the amassed information stored in a droid's data bank?

JEDI MASTER BONUS #6

Identify the servomechanism that rendered droids with the capability to move about.

---

38. What were the devices that essentially served as "eyes" for most droid units?

39. These ambulatory, box-shaped automatons carried an energy-producing generator in their bodies. What type of service droids were they?

40. (Fill in the Blank) Program _____ were internal commands placed in a droid's principal performance banks to create a power overload and generate in the process a moderate-sized but lethal detonation.

41. What was the primary mechanism within a droid that transmogrified energy into automation?

42. (True or False) Only those droids whose principal purpose was to continually interface and interact with organic beings were furnished with speech synthesizers.

43. What secret information was R2-D2 carrying in his memory bank in *Star Wars*?

JEDI MASTER BONUS #7

What type of droid models could expand and intensify the computer capabilities of spacecraft by plugging into terminals or ship-interface receptacles?

---

44. (True or False) Third-degree droids were classified by their skills in security and military applications.

45. Which degree of droid classifications was the domain of the social sciences and service areas such as diplomatic assistance?
    A. First degree
    B. Second degree
    C. Third degree

46. What did C-3PO say was his first job?

47. What did R2-D2 state was responsible for short-circuiting his holographic recording system in *Star Wars: A New Hope*?
    A. The restraining bolt
    B. A defective photoreceptor
    C. Carbon scoring

48. What type of droid self-destructed in *The Empire Strikes Back* in order to avoid capture?

49. At the end of *Star Wars: A New Hope*, what was C-3PO willing to donate if it would assist in R2-D2's repairs?

JEDI MASTER BONUS #8

According to C-3PO in *The Empire Strikes Back*, what were the approximate odds of surviving a trip through an asteroid belt?

---

50. How many mechanical appendages, or "legs," did the Imperial probot have that Han Solo destroyed on Hoth?
    A. Four
    B. Five
    C. Six

51. According to R2-D2, what were the odds against Luke and Han's survival on the frozen tundra of Hoth?
    A. 1001:1
    B. 964:1
    C. 725:1

52. (True or False) R2-D2's dome-shaped head could turn a full three hundred and sixty degrees.

53. What did the other 3PO droid unit say to See-Threepio in the corridor of Cloud City?
    A. "Ke chu to!"
    B. "E chu Ta!"
    C. "O ta cha!"

54. What was the color of R2-D2's trim?

55. (Fill in the blank dialogue) The primary function of a power droid was the " _____ up" of other droids, vessels, vehicles, and other mechanical devices.

56. How many photoreceptors did R2-D2 have?

JEDI MASTER BONUS #9

How many meters in height was R2-D2?

---

57. Which of the following was NOT one of R2-D2's many retractable maintenance appendages hidden within his short, squat, cylindrical body?
    A. Grasping claws
    B. Circular saws
    C. Surgical apparatus

58. How did Jawas load droids aboard their huge, multistoried sandcrawler transports?

59. In *Star Wars: A New Hope,* what did Luke Skywalker and Ben Kenobi discover in the desert of Tatooine to make them suspect that R2-D2 and C-3PO were being tracked by Imperial troops?

60. (True or False) When the nomadic Sand People attacked Luke Skywalker, C-3PO lost his right arm.

61. (True or False) R2-D2 stood perpendicular on two appendages that ended in treaded rollers, but a third "leg" (which dropped from a lower body compartment) allowed him to "walk" across uneven and rough topography.

62. What mistake did Chewie make when he reconstructed a dismembered C-3PO?

63. (True or False) C-3PO was sometimes referred to as the "Professor."

JEDI MASTER BONUS #10

R2-D2 was classified as an astromech droid, but what was his robot classification?

JEDI MASTER BONUS #11

In *The Empire Strikes Back*, identify the sector of the Rebel base and the direction in which the Imperial probot was conducting its reconnaissance mission.

BEHIND-THE-SCENES
Star Wars: A New Hope

1. How many models were used in the production of the movie?
   A. 50
   B. 100
   C. 150

2. (True or False) The sound of Darth Vader's labored breathing was achieved with a house painter's filtered spray mask.

3. What did the special effects technicians line the bottom of Luke Skywalker's landspeeder with to make the vehicle appear suspended above the ground?

4. The origin of droid R2-D2's name came from a small phrase of film editor's lexicon. What is the abbreviation R2-D2 short for in that particular jargon?

5. In which popular science-fiction film did special effects technicians include an upside down R2-D2 in the detail of a large, mother spacecraft as homage to *Star Wars: A New Hope*?
   A. *Independence Day*
   B. *E.T.*
   C. *Close Encounters of the Third Kind*

6. (True or False) George Lucas created Industrial Light & Magic in 1975 because he couldn't find an outside company to do the special effects for *Star Wars: A New Hope*.

JEDI MASTER BONUS #1

What was the length and height of the full-scale model of the *Millennium Falcon*?

---

7. Who were most of the extras in the film's final scene in which the Rebel heroes received their medallions from Princess Leia?
   A. Family members of the film crew
   B. Cardboard cutouts
   C. Union laborers on strike from a nearby construction site

8. Which Japanese words (translated to mean "period drama") served as the inspiration for the word "Jedi"?
   A. *Jidai Geki*
   B. *Jeda Geki*
   C. *Jeki Diga*

9. (Fill in the Blank) Most of the movie was shot by vintage 1950s _____ cameras because they were of higher quality than any others available at the time.

10. George Lucas modeled Obi-Wan Kenobi after a Samurai warrior, and C-3PO and R2-D2's origin was a couple of petty criminals the warrior drafted to help him rescue a princess in distress. Identify the Japanese movie that influenced Lucas' *Star Wars* character development.
    A. *Sword of the Samurai*
    B. *Ancient Warriors*
    C. *Hidden Fortress*

11. Which actress was Lucas' second choice for the role of Princess Leia?

A. Nancy Allen
B. Amy Irving
C. Jodie Foster

12. (True or False) The movie's spacecraft were made from every-thing from model race car and motorcycle kits to the egg-shaped plastic containers for women's stockings.

JEDI MASTER BONUS #2

Which scene of the movie was the first ever to be produced by Lucas' Industrial Light & Magic's (ILM) special effects magicians?

---

13. Identify the Hollywood union group that attempted to "order" Lucas to recut the movie and insert credits at the beginning.

14. Who or what served as a model of inspiration for the creation of the Chewbacca character?

15. (True or False) Cardboard cutouts were utilized for some of the background starfighters in the Rebel hangar bay scenes.

16. Which actor held his breath for so long during the trash com-pactor scene aboard the Death Star that he broke a blood ves-sel in his face and subsequent shots were filmed from one side only?
    A. Harrison Ford
    B. Mark Hamill
    C. Peter Mayhew

17. (True or False) Mark Hamill deliberately didn't learn his lines for the intercom conversation in the cell block scene so that it would sound spontaneous.

18. What was shown hanging in the cockpit of the *Millennium Falcon* as Chewbacca prepared to depart from the Mos Eisley spaceport, but did not appear in succeeding scenes?
    - A. A pair of dice
    - B. A model of *Star Trek*'s original *Enterprise*
    - C. A small photo of Harrison Ford's wife, Melissa, who wrote the screenplay for *E.T.*

JEDI MASTER BONUS #3

In the original version of *Star Wars: A New Hope*, Luke Skywalker's landspeeder rode rather than glided into the Mos Eisley spaceport, but in the *Special Edition* release in 1997, the computer graphics team at ILM reworked the scene to make the vehicle appear as if it was actually floating above the terrain. What else did Lucas add to that particular scene in *Star Wars: The Special Edition*?

---

19. Identify the classic movie whose robot's art deco lines inspired the design for C-3PO?
    - A. *It Came From Outer Space*
    - B. *Invading Robots from Mars*
    - C. *Metropolis*

20. (True or False) James Earl Jones supplied the voice for Darth Vader, but specifically requested that he not receive on-screen credit because he felt that his work on the film was minimal.

21. In which lush, tropical country was the Rebel's Yavin base filmed?
    - A. Honduras
    - B. Panama
    - C. Guatemala

22. Name the record company that distributed the soundtrack for *Star Wars: A New Hope*.

23. Who did most of the preliminary sketches prior to the movie's actual filming?
    A. George Lucas
    B. Ralph McQuarrie
    C. Rick McCallum

24. According to George Lucas, from which two characters' points of views is *Star Wars: A New Hope* told?
    A. Obi-Wan Kenobi and Luke Skywalker
    B. R2-D2 and C-3PO
    C. Luke Skywalker and Princess Leia

JEDI MASTER BONUS #4

Who was the chief model builder for *Star Wars*?

---

25. The *Star Wars* saga as originally conceived by George Lucas was much too expansive to be made into a single movie or even a cinematic trilogy, so Lucas structured his creative ideas into three trilogies. Why did he elect to film the middle trilogy first?

26. (True or False) Modified Sterling 9mm submachine guns were actually used as the movie's laser rifles.

27. Which form of martial arts did Lucas draw inspiration from when forming the basics of the Force?
    A. Aikido
    B. Tai Chi
    C. Kung Fu

28. Which character's last name officially changed spelling between the time of *Star Wars: A New Hope* and *Return of the Jedi*?

29. Who was the costume designer for *Star Wars: A New Hope*?

A. Debra Broide
B. John Mollo
C. Tracy Bernstein

JEDI MASTER BONUS #5

Limited by time, budget, and technology, Lucas was never fully satisfied with the initial version of *Star Wars: A New Hope.* In *The Special Edition*, with the assistance of a team from ILM, he was able to add and replace scenes to make the science-fiction classic more visually exciting. In the original film, a *Millennium Falcon* model was used in the shot of the freighter escaping from the Mos Eisley spaceport, but in *The Special Edition* version a computer-generated *Falcon* took to the desert skies of Tatooine. What else did ILM technicians add to the scene?

---

30. Who were the film editors for *Star Wars: A New Hope*?
    A. Paul Hirsch, Marcia Lucas and Richard Chew
    B. Sue Harke, Ruben Macias and Ian Spelling
    C. Jack Bergstrom, Dick Dahlquist and Carla Grayson

31. (True or False) Filming for *Star Wars: A New Hope* first began in the barren desert of Tunisia in North Africa in October 1976.

32. Why did production supervisor Robert Watts and production designer John Barry choose Tunisia over Morocco as the location site for filming the Tatooine scenes?

33. This noted artist designed the powerful and distinctive posters for such blockbusters as *E.T.*, *The Lion King, Cocoon, Batman Forever, Blade Runner*, and the packaging for the international distribution of the *Star Wars* videocassette trilogy released in 1995–96. What is this movie advertising designer's name?

A. Ed Echols
B. Bryan Grayson
C. John Alvin

34. When Fox Home Entertainment rereleased a box set of the *Star Wars* trilogy in 1995, the VHS tapes were the first ones ever to be digitally mastered using Lucasfilm's THX Mastering Process, which ensured that the quality of the videos' sound and picture were as close to the quality of the original motion pictures as possible. What does THX stand for, and what is the relationship between the sound system's inventor and George Lucas?

35. Which orchestra performed the music for *Star Wars: A New Hope*?
    A. The New York Philharmonic
    B. The London Symphony
    C. The Boston Pops

JEDI MASTER BONUS #6

Originally *Star Wars: The Special Edition* was to be nothing more than a restoration project, but during the process George Lucas realized that he could change, enhance or add some scenes that were technically impossible in 1977. Where were additional shots filmed in which Imperial stormtroopers arrived on Tatooine?

---

36. Which star of the movie has said repeatedly in interviews, "I was desperate to do *Star Wars* because it was the best script I had seen, it was a fairy tale"?
    A. Mark Hamill
    B. Anthony Daniels
    C. Carrie Fisher

37. Who recommended and introduced composer John Williams (who eventually scored *Star Wars: A New Hope*) to Lucas?

38. Which single word has George Lucas said sums up his involvement in the "whole *Star Wars* experience"?
    A. "Phenomenal"
    B. "Unpredictable"
    C. "Fun"

39. (True or False) Lucas has acknowledged that the "original impetus" of *Star Wars* was a serial called *Adventure Theatre: Flash Gordon Conquers the Universe.*

40. Which two movie studios passed on *Star Wars: A New Hope* before Lucas finally sold the film to 20ᵗʰ Century Fox?
    A. United Artists and Universal
    B. Paramount and Disney
    C. Warner Brothers and Columbia

41. Although Harrison Ford had costarred in Lucas' *American Graffiti*, which skilled but menial labor job was he working at when Lucas asked him to read for the part of Han Solo?
    A. Plumber
    B. Carpenter
    C. Painter

JEDI MASTER BONUS #7

How much of *Star Wars: A New Hope*'s $10 million budget was used for the movie's special effects?

---

42. (True or False) The average age of the F/X technicians hired to work on *Star Wars: A New Hope* was twenty-one.

43. Casting with the same approach he used on *American Graffiti*, Lucas chose new, fresh talent for three of the five major roles

in *Star Wars: A New Hope.* Identify the two veterans of the British screen Lucas cast as characters in the movie.

44. (True or False) Lucas felt that the movie was so original and so highly different in all of its physical orientations—unknown creatures, strange new worlds, and noises previously unheard of—that the music should be on a fairly familiar emotional level, not electronic but an almost nineteenth century romantic, symphonic score against this new galaxy far, far away. . . .

45. George Lucas has commented about *The Special Edition*, "The digital technology that ILM (Industrial Light and Magic) has pioneered in films like *Jurassic Park* and *Forrest Gump* allows me to revise a few scenes which will bring the movie closer to my original vision." The technology also allowed Lucas to complete the scene in which Han Solo confronted Jabba the Hutt, partially filmed in 1976, but not included in the original film. Approximately how many minutes of both live-action and computer-animated footage was added to *Star Wars: The Special Edition*?

46. What was the worldwide theatrical gross of the original version of *Star Wars: A New Hope*?
    A. $400 million
    B. $475 million
    C. $513 million

47. (Fill in the blank with the correct number) In *The Special Edition*, there was a _____ -frame delay on the wings of the X-wing starfighters popping open as they approached the Death Star.

JEDI MASTER BONUS #8

Most of the footage of Tatooine in *Star Wars: A New Hope* was shot in the deserts of the North Africa country of Tunisia. Correctly match the numbered black circles on the map with the location scenes from the movie.

_____Mos Eisley

_____Dune Sea

_____Jundland Wastes

_____Homestead courtyard

_____Homestead exterior

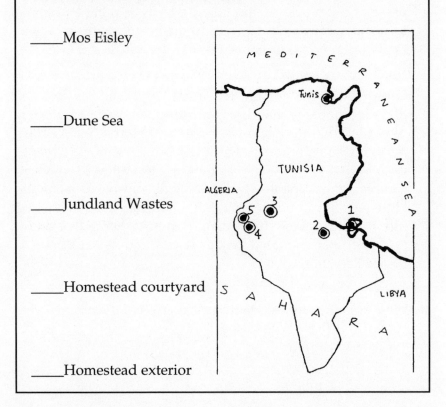

48. During the early stages of storyline conception and preproduction for *Star Wars: A New Hope*, what was Luke's original name before it was eventually changed to Skywalker?

    A. Skyrunner
    B. Starkiller
    C. Moonwalker

49. In 20th Century Fox press releases in early 1977, which character was described as a "barbarous-looking alien giant"?

50. Which three *Star Wars: A New Hope* figures made history by becoming the first fictional characters to leave their prints at the famous Chinese Theater in 1977?
    A. Luke Skywalker, Princess Leia, and Han Solo
    B. Ben Kenobi, Darth Vader, and Luke Skywalker
    C. C-3PO, R2-D2, and Darth Vader

51. Which actor claimed in several interviews for the movie, "I would like to become instantly recognizable"?

52. (True or False) Les Dilley, who went on to become a noted production designer for such films as *Casper, The Abyss, An American Werewolf in London,* and *Raiders of the Lost Ark,* made his mark in the industry as art director for *Star Wars: A New Hope.*

53. Will the *real* producer for *Star Wars: A New Hope* please stand up?
    A. Ronald Mauldin
    B. Nicholas Morrison
    C. Gary Kurtz

54. Who was the diminutive English actor who operated R2-D2 from inside the barrel-shaped body?
    A. Carl Brokaw
    B. Kenny Baker
    C. Cecil Larney

55. (True or False) R2-D2 was essentially developed from George Lucas' sketches.

56. (Fill in the Blank) Originally, the F/X crew had planned on achieving the brilliant effects of the Jedi lightsaber by utilizing a 3M manufactured substance known as _____, the

highly light-reflective material that made road signs amplify light and appear brightly.

57. (True or False) Although out of the sight of the movie's viewers, the set decorators hung a tiny *Star Wars* poster and a *Playboy* centerfold on the cockpit walls of Princess Leia's Rebel Blockade Runner as a movie-making "in-joke."

JEDI MASTER BONUS #9

How many of the movie's original 100+ F/X shots were entirely redone for *The Special Edition* version, using current computer-generated image (CGI) technology?

JEDI MASTER BONUS #10

One major "new" scene for *The Special Edition* involved the Empire's search for C-3PO and R2-D2's escape pod on Tatooine. Identify the five computer-generated images added to the scene's live-footage shots.

JEDI MASTER BONUS #11

What was the difference between the dewbacks in the original *Star Wars* and the ones in *The Special Edition* version?

---

58. Identify the *Star Wars* writer who adapted the first film for a National Public Radio serial dramatization.
    A. Timothy Zahn
    B. Dave Wolverton
    C. Brian Dailey

59. Which national publication profiled the movie on its July 18, 1977, cover with the teaser: "*Star Wars:* The Talented Folks (All under 40) Who Gave Us C-3PO and the Summer's Box Office Sizzler"?

A. *People*
B. *Life*
C. *Time*

60. Which actor later acknowledged in interviews that he would not have taken the role in the movie if he had known how uncomfortably "torturous" his costume was going to be during filming?

61. (True or False) George Lucas had difficulty in obtaining funding to film *Star Wars: A New Hope* because most studios strongly believed that audiences wouldn't go see a "quirky science-fiction movie."

62. Rather than the orchestra-performed soundtrack, which scene in the movie was the only one to incorporate its own source music?

63. Identify the international beverage, snack and fast-food giant that became partners with Lucasfilms to promote *The Special Editions* with all its brands in a single global marketing effort.

64. (True or False) C-3PO actor Anthony Daniels could not take his mask off during the first day of filming for *Star Wars: A New Hope,* and was forced to drink through a straw.

JEDI MASTER BONUS #12

What was the total cost of *The Special Edition*'s enhanced special effects, print restoration, digitally remastered soundtracks and new footage?

---

65. What explanation did Lucas give for deleting the Han Solo/Jabba the Hutt encounter from the original version?

66. In 1978, *The Star Wars Holiday Special* aired for its only showing, which revolved around Chewie visiting his family on his

homeworld. Although most of the major movie characters had cameos, which minor *Star Wars* figure appeared in a short cartoon during the telecast?

67. (Fill in the blank with the correct movie title) George Lucas and director Brian DePalma held an immense, joint casting call for young women in 1976. Lucas was searching for an actress to play Princess Leia, the only major female character in *Star Wars: A New Hope,* and DePalma was looking for a young woman to star in _____ , the first cinematic adaptation of a Stephen King novel.

68. What reason did Carrie Fisher give for "sounding English" during most of her lines in *Star Wars: A New Hope*?
    A. Lucas told her she would sound more "princesslike" and "regal"
    B. She had just returned from school in England
    C. Her mother, actress Debbie Reynolds, advised her to speak like Queen Elizabeth

69. Identify the F/X wizard of *Alien* and *Terminator* fame who was responsible for the creatures in *The Star Wars Holiday Special.*

70. (True or False) The appearance of the subtitle *Episode IV: A New Hope* was on new prints struck for the two-week reissue of *Star Wars* on April 10, 1981, almost one year after the premiere of *The Empire Strikes Back.*

71. (True or False) Even though George Lucas' *American Graffiti* had grossed over $115 million at the box office, for his next movie, *Star Wars,* Lucas abandoned demands for a larger salary and instead insisted on ownership of the merchandising, music, publishing rights, and all sequels.

JEDI MASTER BONUS #13

Identify the porno actress originally cast as Camie, a local Tatooine girl in the infamous cut scene between Luke Skywalker and Biggs Darklighter.

---

72. (Fill in the blank with the correct number) When a 70mm version of *Star Wars* was released on May 25, 1977, it was shown in only _____ theaters in nine cities.

73. Whose daughters appeared in the movie disguised as Jawas?
    A. Mark Hamill's
    B. George Lucas'
    C. Harrison Ford's

74. Which scene did Carrie Fisher describe in an interview as "the most awful day of filming on the set," although she was extremely "pissed" to discover later that it was cut from the final version of the movie?

75. According to a *Rolling Stone* interview with George Lucas, how did he come up with the name of *Star Wars'* archvillain, Darth Vader?

76. (True or False) A scene was filmed but later cut in which Luke Skywalker met someone in the Rebel hangar that knew his father.

77. According to Carrie Fisher, which three words did George Lucas repeatedly scream at her while she filmed her scenes for *Star Wars: A New Hope*?
    A. "Move, move, move"
    B. "Smile, frown, squint"
    C. "Faster, more intense"

78. What were the names of Chewie's wife, father and son in the 1978 *Star Wars Holiday Special*?
    A. Caquala, Takar and Uno
    B. Mala, Itchy and Lumpy
    C. Wyto, Klondo and Grotto

79. (Fill in the blank with the correct movie title) The species name "Wookiee" originated during the filming of _____, when an actor ad-libbed background dialogue with the line, "It sounds like you ran over a Wookiee back there!"

JEDI MASTER BONUS #14

According to George Lucas, the Wookiee Chewbacca was largely based upon his pet malamute, Indiana. But what was the origin of the name "Chewbacca"?

JEDI MASTER BONUS #15

Identify the 1996 movie that was the first film to run the 2-minute and 20-second promotional trailer which opened with the image of a small TV screen and a voice that said, "For an entire generation people have experienced *Star Wars* this way . . . On Presidents' Day weekend, 1997, see the *Star Wars* trilogy again for the first time"?

THE NAME GAME
Star Wars: A New Hope

Match the name of the actor with the corresponding character he or she portrayed in the first installment of the Star Wars *trilogy.*

---

1. _____	Phil Brown	A.	General Tagge
2. _____	Shelagh Fraser	B.	Chief Jawa
3. _____	Jack Purvis	C.	Wedge Antilles
4. _____	Alex McCrindle	D.	Admiral Motti
5. _____	Eddie Byrne	E.	Owen Lars
6. _____	Dennis Lawson	F.	Porkins
7. _____	Leslie Schofield	G.	General Dodonna
8. _____	Richard Le Parmentier	H.	Beru Lars
9. _____	Don Henderson	I.	John D
10. _____	William Hootkins	J.	Biggs Darklighter
11. _____	Garrick Hagon	K.	Commander Willard
12. _____	Jack Klaff	L.	Imperial Commander #1

STAR TECH

From repulsorlift engines to particle shielding, from alluvial dampers to hyperdrive motivators, from horizontal boosters to fusioncutters, this trivia quiz will determine how knowledgeable you are about Star Wars' *full spectrum of awesome technology. (WARNING: Immediate disqualification will result if you sneak a peek at the* Star Wars Technical Journal.)

────────────────────

1. Identify the electro-optical devices that recorded the thumbprints of buyers and sellers throughout the galaxy, thus officially documenting property and merchandise transactions.

2. (Fill in the Blank) A starship's alluvial _____ regulated the craft's amount of thrust by blocking the emission of ion particles.

3. What did a starship have to engage before it was able to exceed the speed of light?

4. Identify the holographic projection table primarily used for recreational purposes aboard the stock freighter *Millennium Falcon*.

5. (Fill in the Blank) Small repulsor projectors known as _____ were used to control and influence pitch in a starship.

6. What type of generators produced the power required to originate and sustain deflector shields?

JEDI MASTER BONUS #1

In how many locations was the tractor beam coupled to the Death Star's main reactor in *Star Wars: A New Hope*?

---

7. What was a starship's most powerful onboard engine and principal propelling force?

8. In starfighters, where were the pressor activators located?
    A. On helm control consoles
    B. In the control sticks
    C. Directly below the arming mechanism

9. (Fill in the Blank) Personal communication transceivers known as _____ were built into the helmets of Imperial stormtroopers.

10. What was spacer lexicon for the divestiture of energy in a ship's power plants?
    A. Brownout
    B. Blackout
    C. Burnout

11. (True or False) Carbonite, a strong admixture of metallic substances, was utilized as a preservative for Tibanna gas.

12. What was the chief light-speed thrust producer in a starship's hyperdrive engine and interrelating systems?
    A. Hyperdrive motivator
    B. Hyperdrive initiator
    C. Hyperdrive calibrator

JEDI MASTER BONUS #2

According to Han Solo, what was the *Millennium Falcon*'s top supralight speed?

---

13. This minute welding instrument was designed especially for repairs of a starship's durable composite metals. Identify this tool.

14. What was the name designation for the parabolic holoprojector array utilized in command centers by both Rebel Alliance and Imperial forces?

15. (Fill in the Blank) Space vessels were able to achieve sublight speeds in normal space by engaging _____ engines.

16. (True or False) Powered by fusion generators, a starship's hyperdrive engine and its interconnected systems were required to catapult the craft to faster-than-light speeds.

17. Identify the hydraulic piston that elevated and lowered the *Millennium Falcon*'s boarding ramp.

18. What was the Blockade Runner's engine complement?

JEDI MASTER BONUS #3

In *The Empire Strikes Back,* what two hand-held tools did Han Solo use to make repairs to the *Millennium Falcon*?

---

19. What was the most popular antigravitational propulsion system, used throughout the galaxy?

20. (Fill in the Blank) Spacecraft utilized landing _____ to attach themselves either magnetically or mechanically to another vessel or a space dock.

21. Identify the devices used by moisture farmers on the desert world of Tatooine to absorb water from the atmosphere.
    A. Macroirrigaters
    B. Vaporators
    C. Moisture inducers

22. (Fill in the Blank) A starship's _____ system was an aggregation of the hyperdrive's opto-electronic and mechanical subsystems.

23. What was the term used for a starship's return to realspace from hyperspace?

24. Identify the diminutive, baseball-size metal remote, blanketed with a matrix of impalpable sensors, that was used as a training tool by military and security personnel.

25. What action did Chewbacca take to force the *Millennium Falcon* out of hyperspace as it approached Alderaan?

26. Which specialized processing unit on the *Millennium Falcon* did Han Solo use to calculate the coordinates for the jump to hyperspace?
    A. Central astrogation chart
    B. Trajectory computer
    C. Navicomputer

JEDI MASTER BONUS #4

In *The Empire Strikes Back*, how often did the crew of the *Millennium Falcon* attempt to engage the hyperdrive and fail, and during which scenes?

JEDI MASTER BONUS #5

Which subsystem components did Han Solo check on the *Falcon* the first time the hyperdrive failed to propel the ship to supralight speed?

---

27. Identify the intercept course trajectory generated by a ship's navicomputer.

28. What portable life-support device was built into Darth Vader's armor?

29. Identify the experimental defensive system that was too costly to install on anything larger than a starfighter.

30. What were the radarlike sensor sweeps used by Imperial forces?
    A. Com-scans
    B. Compact Energy Detectors
    C. Com-sigs

31. How many engines were employed on a Star Destroyer?
    A. Two
    B. Three
    C. Four

32. What was the other widely used term for hyperspace?

JEDI MASTER BONUS #6

Name the three uses of an Imperial Star Destroyer's bottom hatch.

---

33. Identify the cylindrical shaft that served as the transport device for people and objects in building structures, space vessels and space stations throughout the galaxy.

34. (True or False) The readout data displayed within the viewplates of macrobinoculars provided information on the observed object's relative azimuth, range and promontory.

35. (Fill in the Blank) A protective _____ shielding force field deflected matter of any form from starships and planetary structures.

36. Identify the ignition system for a starship.

37. Which device manipulated the massive amounts of energy that surged through a starship's paralight system? A power coupling or a power terminal?

38. What was the metal-analyzing device that Darth Vader used to torture Han Solo on Cloud City?
    A. Thermal scan
    B. Electro-magnetic grid
    C. Scan grid

39. Identify the emitting tower that produced an immobilizing modified force field.
    A. Tractor-beam projector
    B. Tracomp
    C. High intensity deflector shield

40. This propulsion system could only be utilized when an immense gravity mass was in close proximity. Name this starship or speeder propelling force.

JEDI MASTER BONUS #7

What was another name for a thermal coil or warming unit?

---

41. What type of metal was impervious to intensely excessive temperatures and the stress and strain of mechanized operations?

    A. Flexisteel
    B. Durasteel
    C. Permametal

42. What was the other name for high-voltage force pikes?

43. (Fill in the Blank) Highly intense diversion shields known as deflection _____ served as the foundation for most planets' defense systems.

44. This electro-optical device had much greater power and pixel density than electrobinoculars. What was this hand-held viewing apparatus?

45. (True or False) The antiturbulence control aboard space vessels was a computer-enhanced system employed to counterbalance the effects of atmospheric perturbation.

46. Identify the remote-operated force fields employed by detention facilities and other high-security centers to manage right of entry.
    A. Access shields
    B. Static fields
    C. Energy gates

JEDI MASTER BONUS #8

What was the code number for the Death Star's trash compactor in which Luke Skywalker and Company were trapped in *Star Wars: A New Hope*?

---

47. What were the power-producing devices that by generating heat and light were able to recharge the energy cells of droids, weapons and vehicles?

48. Name the powered hand tool used to tighten and loosen screws and bolts.

49. Identify the propulsion engines used to furnish the moving thrust for speeder bikes, airspeeders, and landspeeders.
    A. Propulsionlift enhancers
    B. Pressor propulsors
    C. Repulsors

50. (True or False) Land and atmospheric vehicles could be brought to an energy distribution station for recharging.

51. What was the name of the process that transformed translucent materials such as glass and transparisteel into light filters while maintaining their transparency?

52. Identify the type of force field used on starfighters to impede and assimilate energy fire.
    A. Ray shielding
    B. Repulsor shielding
    C. Particle shielding

53. (True or False) A hyperspanner was a hand-held power tool similar to a wrench.

54. What was the hyperdrive subsystem aboard the *Millennium Falcon* that furnished energy to the ionization compartment to create ignition?

55. (True or False) Holographic recording mode was the procedure for capturing visual images and audio sound bites in a three-dimensional format.

JEDI MASTER BONUS #9

Identify the hand-held tool, carried on all starships, that produced wide-dispersion laser beams.

---

56. What were the wings on an X-wing fighter called?

A. S-foils
B. X-foils
C. THX-foils

57. How many holomonster playing pieces were used in the hologame Chewie and the droids played on the *Millennium Falcon* in *Star Wars: A New Hope*?
    A. 8
    B. 10
    C. 12

58. Identify the device Luke used to view the battle between the Rebel Blockade Runner and the Star Destroyer.

59. Which optical instrument was utilized by Rebel officers on Hoth?
    A. Electrorangefinder
    B. Electrobinoculars
    C. Electrotelescope

60. What kept Cloud City suspended over the gas-giant planet Bespin?

JEDI MASTER BONUS #10

Identify the component in a spacecraft's hyperdrive engine system that determined jump thrusts, calibrated engine performance in hyperspace, and regulated safe returns to normal space.

ALIEN FACES & PLACES
Part I

The far, far away galaxy of Star Wars *has always been known for its myriad life forms of virtually every imaginable design, shape and size, emanating from equally fascinating and varied alien worlds throughout the universe. Who were those strange beings who patronized the cantina at Mos Eisley spaceport? From what exotic locales or desolate worlds did the aliens in Jabba the Hutt's notorious criminal lair originate? Test your knowledge of alien faces and places with the following trivia questions.*

1. Who were the humanoid-porcine beings who formed the work force in the Tibanna-gas processing plants on the floating Cloud City above Bespin?

2. (True or False) Because of their ability to withstand extremely hot and humid climates, large repitilian dewbacks were often used by moisture farmers on Tatooine in place of automated vehicles.

3. Identify the meter-tall scavenger race on Tatooine who traveled in bands, searching for hardware or crashed spacecraft to steal or salvage.

4. Name the Nikto skiff guard with green reptilian skin and small horns who worked at Jabba the Hutt's palace.

    A. Traco
    B. Draxx
    C. Klaatu

5. Identify the ten-meter long, tentacled creature that tried to eat Luke Skywalker in the refuse of the original Death Star's watery waste disposal.

6. Who was one of Bail Organa's most loyal and trustworthy servants on Alderaan?
    A. Tarrik
    B. Beton
    C. G'eevender

JEDI MASTER BONUS #1

In *Star Wars: A New Hope,* where did Luke Skywalker tell his uncle Owen he was going to obtain some power converters?

---

7. (True or False) The twin stars of the Tatooine system were Trilo I and Trilo II.

8. Identify the white-furred carnivorous beast that attacked Luke Skywalker by surprise while he was on patrol on the frozen tundra of the Hoth planet.

9. What was the name of the spaceport city on the Outer Rim world of Tatooine that Ben Kenobi referred to as a "hive of scum and villainy"?

10. Which race of warriors was defeated by the Jedi Knights during the Clone Wars?
    A. Calamarian
    B. Huton
    C. Mandalore

11. Name the blue, floppy-eared Ortolan musician who with his jizz-wailer band often played exclusively for Jabba the Hutt at his palace on Tatooine.

12. Identify the largely deserted star system adjacent to the Hoth system in which Han Solo and his *Millennium Falcon* were able to hide from pursing Imperial Star Destroyers.
    A. J'kara
    B. Anoat
    C. Lyytex

JEDI MASTER BONUS #2

Name the alien world that was infamous for its planet-wide Imperial prison and impenetrable defenses.

---

13. (True or False) L'lash was a delicacy indigenous to the planet Endor.

14. (True or False) The ancient and massive temples of Massassi were located on the fourth moon of Yavin.

15. They had small horns extending from their foreheads and multiple nostrils on their flat faces. Identify this humanoid species, several of whom were employed as skiff guards for crime lord Jabba the Hutt.

16. (Fill in the Blank) An asteroid-dwelling, 900-meter-long, wormlike space _____ swallowed the *Millennium Falcon* in *The Empire Strikes Back*.

17. Name the yellow-green skinned and spotted lead singer for the jizz-wailing band in Jabba the Hutt's palace who sang through an elongated mouth.

18. Identify the bipedal pachydermoid gangster who was a criminal associate of Jabba the Hutt.
    A. Ephant Mon
    B. Lazquer Yei
    C. Vetox Kaameer

JEDI MASTER BONUS #3

Describe what Imperial forces discovered on Dantooine in *Star Wars: A New Hope.*

---

19. Which planet did the flesh-eating gravel-maggots inhabit?
    A. Tatooine
    B. Gargon
    C. Kamar

20. Name the sixth planet in the Hoth star system.

21. Identify the rodentlike species with foul body odor and jabbering speech who traveled and lived within massive sand vehicles on Tatooine.

22. Which planet was entirely destroyed by the Galactic Empire as an exhibition of the original Death Star's awesome annihilative capabilities?

23. Name the beastly quadrupeds used by moisture farmers on the flat deserts of Tatooine and as pack animals by the Sand People.

24. Which planet sympathetic to the Alliance harbored a covert Rebel base?
    A. Graffeine
    B. Bestine
    C. Iopa

JEDI MASTER BONUS #4

Name the species whose far-reaching intelligence-gathering network located the site of the Empire's second Death Star battle station.

25. In which Mos Eisley docking bay did the *Millennium Falcon* rendezvous with Luke Skywalker, Ben Kenobi and the R2-D2 and C-3PO droids?
    A. 45
    B. 76
    C. 94

26. To which species did the pudgy, jizz-wailing musician Droopy McCool belong?

27. What was the name of the large sand pit in the wastes of Tatooine's Dune Sea where the gargantuan and multitentacled creature known as Sarlacc resided?

28. Identify the four-armed animal species well-respected through-out the galaxy for its courage and astounding strength.
    A. Lapsoid
    B. Gundark
    C. Yaztec

29. (True or False) Cooler was one of crime lord Jabba the Hutt's alien subordinates.

30. This Nikto piloted one of Jabba's skiffs and was killed during Luke Skywalker's rescue of Han Solo and Princess Leia. Who was this alien?

JEDI MASTER BONUS #5

What color was a Bespin guard's uniform and hat?

---

31. Identify the planet that was conquered by Imperial forces after it was discovered that it was one of the Alliance's original allies in the Galactic Civil War.
    A. Ralltiir
    B. Beto
    C. Aanukkah

32. What type of large and fearsome repitilian beast did Luke Skywalker destroy when Jabba the Hutt dropped the Jedi Knight into a special pit below the gangster's court in his palace on Tatooine?
    A. Rampa
    B. Rancor
    C. Ranat

33. (True or False) Sanctuary Moon was one of the names attributed to Endor's forested planetary satellite.

34. What was the other name for the aggressive and nomadic Sand People of Tatooine?

35. Identify the vicious and carnivorous rodents that Luke Skywalker hunted while flying his skyhopper through the rugged and twisting canyons of Tatooine at high speed.
    A. Womp rats
    B. Quinetine bats
    C. Reliaan parcas

36. What was the name of the six-breasted girl who entertained Jabba the Hutt and his criminal associates by dancing in the court of his desert palace?

A. Gamor
B. Sylethian
C. Gargan

JEDI MASTER BONUS #6

An Alliance convoy was destroyed and its crew killed in a
surprise attack by Imperial forces near this planet in the
Derra star system.

---

37. Which remote and isolated planet once harbored the Alliance's
    operations base?
    A. Haedon
    B. Dantooine
    C. Daluuj

38. Name the planet that served as an outlying settlement and port
    of call for spacecraft traveling the trade runs near the Corel-
    lian star system.
    A. Commenor
    B. Jadis II
    C. Sterylax Quor

39. Who was the Alderaanian consular who commanded the *Tan-
    tive IV*?

40. Name the creature with amphibious eyes and elongated, pro-
    truding lower teeth that was a pet of a Jawa tribe on Tatooine.

41. Identify the alien race more commonly known throughout the
    galaxy as Head Hunters.
    A. Amanaman
    B. Tammuud
    C. Behanian

42. (True or False) Han Solo was Corellian, a humanoid race of be-
    ings that inhabited the Corellia star system.

JEDI MASTER BONUS #7

What color were the structures in Cloud City's business and
residential sections?

---

43. Name the immense, carnivorous reptiles that lived in the
    mountain terrain encompassing the Jundland Wastes of
    Tatooine.

44. Meerian Hammerhead belonged to which alien class of hu-
    manoids with flat heads and bowed necks?
    A. N'laxians
    B. Ithorians
    C. Xexothians

45. What was the name of the Mon Calamari's homeworld?

46. Identify the dark, winged creatures whose suction organs pro-
    vided them with the ability to attach themselves to traveling
    spacecraft and feed off the ships' energy.
    A. Kykrs
    B. Mynocks
    C. Praedors

47. What was the name for the diminutive night-loving arthro-
    pods indigenous to Tatooine?

48. This enchanting Twi'lek slave girl was dropped into the Ran-
    cor pit by Jabba the Hutt when she disobeyed the sluglike
    crime lord. What was her name?

JEDI MASTER BONUS #8

What was the collective name for the star systems located on the outermost boundary of Imperial space?

---

49. In *Star Wars: A New Hope*, what did Luke Skywalker and Ben Kenobi do with the dead Jawas?

50. Why were Luke Skywalker and Artoo-Detoo suspicious when they arrived at the Cloud City mining outpost and trading station in *The Empire Strikes Back*?

51. Identify the alien creature with widely spaced eyes, colossal nostrils and a broad smile who appeared in the Mos Eisley cantina during Luke, Ben and Han's clandestine meeting.
    A. Momaw Nadon
    B. Labria
    C. Snaggletooth

52. (Fill in the blank dialogue) When Han Solo sliced open the dead Tauntaun in *The Empire Strikes Back*, he mumbled to himself, "I thought they smelled _____ on the *outside*."

THE WAN AND OBI:
BEN KENOBI

Imperial Security Bureau (ISB)
Dossier #486719

1. What was Kenobi's rank during the Clone Wars?

2. Who taught the Jedi Knight the ways of the Force?

3. Identify the two other legendary heroes of the Clone Wars who battled alongside Kenobi as they defended the Old Republic?

4. Although Kenobi wasn't experienced as a teacher, who was the pilot he decided to train as a Jedi Knight?

5. What action did Kenobi take when he realized that his good friend and pupil had been corrupted by the dark side of the Force and all his efforts to draw him back had failed?

6. (Fill in the Blank) Kenobi became a hermit and recluse, living in Tatooine's Jundland Wastes, on the _____ edge of the vast desert known as the Dune Sea.

JEDI MASTER BONUS #1

What did Kenobi do to frighten the Tusken Raiders away from Luke Skywalker's landspeeder?

---

7. Who referred to the old Jedi Knight as a "wizard"?

8. How did Kenobi know that Imperial troops, rather than Tatooine Sand People, were tracking the droids C-3PO and R2-D2 across the desert?

9. What did Kenobi place on Luke Skywalker's head when he was training him in the ways of the Force?

10. What was Kenobi's mission on the Imperial Death Star battle station?
    A. Overload the power systems
    B. Power-down the superlaser
    C. Disengage the tractor beam

11. Kenobi provoked Darth Vader into a lightsaber duel in order to provide Luke Skywalker and his companions the time they needed to escape from the Death Star. What warning did Kenobi give the Dark Lord before he gave his life in combat?
    A. "You may strike me down, Vader, but I will return more powerful than ever."
    B. "If you strike me down, I shall become more powerful than you can possibly imagine."
    C. "You may be strong in the dark side of the Force, but if you strike me down, I will come back stronger than you or the Emperor could ever imagine."

12. What remained of Kenobi after Vader struck him down with his lightsaber?

13. What did Vader do to Kenobi's cloak after their death duel ended?

JEDI MASTER BONUS #2

What were Kenobi's first words to Luke Skywalker after his physical being was destroyed by Darth Vader during the lightsaber duel?

---

14. Although he was "with the Force" after his death, Kenobi still played a major role in young Skywalker's life. How many times and where did the old Jedi Knight appear and speak to him in spirit form during the events chronicled in *The Empire Strikes Back*?
    A. Twice: once on Hoth, once on Dagobah
    B. Three times: once on Hoth, twice on Dagobah
    C. Four times: twice on Hoth, twice on Dagobah

15. (Fill in the blank dialogue) After Yoda confirmed Vader's claim that the Dark Lord was indeed Luke Skywalker's father, the young Rebel pilot scolded a shimmering image of Kenobi sitting in the Dagobah bog. However, Kenobi defended his actions by saying, "Your father, Anakin, was _____ by the dark side of the Force—He ceased to be Anakin Skywalker, and became Darth Vader. . . . The good man who was your father was destroyed. So what I told you was true . . . from a certain point of view."

16. What did Kenobi tell Luke to bury "deep down" or they would be made to serve the Emperor?

17. (Fill in the Blank) Before departing to confront his father once again and attempt to turn Vader to the good side of the Force, Luke was warned by Kenobi, "You cannot escape your _____."

JEDI MASTER BONUS #3

What did Kenobi call R2-D2 when he first met the droid on Tatooine?

JEDI MASTER BONUS #4

(Fill in the blank dialogue)

Kenobi described the Force as "what gives a Jedi his power. It flows through us, _____ us, and binds the universe together."

EWOK THIS WAY

The furry, meter-tall Ewoks native to Endor's forest moon were strong in the hunt with their primitive bows and spears, but not warlike, and it was very much out of character for them to become involved in the Galactic Civil War between the Empire and the Rebel Alliance. Nevertheless, they did commit themselves to the Rebel cause, and with their combination of chants, screams, trumpets, drum rhythms, and homeworld advantage, they were able to overcome the Empire's vastly superior communication and war tactics.

---

1. Identify the Ewok who was the first of his tribe to encounter and make friends with Princess Leia after she crashed an Imperial speeder bike and became separated from the Rebel strike force.
   A. Brickett B. Baroque
   B. Wicket W. Warrick
   C. Papos P. Peskins

2. Name the Ewok tribal leader whose striped fur alternated between two shades of gray.
   A. Teebo
   B. Ricket
   C. Jotahr

3. Although primitive warriors, the Ewoks of Endor's moon were able to assist the Rebel strike force in their mission to sabotage the shield generator protecting the unfinished Death

Star. What type of Imperial combat vehicle were the Ewoks especially effective in disabling?

4. Which tan-striped Ewok was the medicine man of the tribe that befriended the Rebel strike team?
    A. Thotay
    B. Korridian
    C. Logray

5. Identify the antiquated method of transportation that the Ewoks used to travel across Endor's moon of vast forests and valleys.

6. (True or False) The Ewoks dwelt in close-knit villages constructed high within the immense trees of Endor's Sanctuary Moon.

JEDI MASTER BONUS #1

Identify the Ewok who stole a speeder bike and effectively diverted the attention of the Imperial soldiers long enough to give the Rebel strike force an opportunity to penetrate the compound housing the Death Star's shield generator.

---

7. (True or False) Wilkey and Nappett were the names of baby Ewoks in the tribe that befriended the Rebels.

8. Identify the governing body among the different Ewok tribes.
    A. Ruling House of Bishops
    B. Council of Elders
    C. Committee of Wise Ones

9. What color was Chief Chirpa's fur?
    A. Gray
    B. Black and white
    C. Brown

10. What did Logray wear atop his furry head?

11. What type of weapon did Teebo carry?
    A. A spear (made from the sharpened bone of a forest creature)
    B. A slingshot (constructed from the dried intestines of a Qipoo bird)
    C. A stone hatchet

12. Name the Ewok who convinced his tribe to assist the Rebels in their mission to disable the Death Star's shield generator.

JEDI MASTER BONUS #2

How many feathers adorned the crest of Logray's headdress?

---

13. (True or False) Chief Chirpa was outfitted with the teeth, horns, tusks, and bones of forest animals he had hunted and killed on Endor's moon.

14. (Fill in the Blank) The Ewoks' medicine man brandished a staff adorned with the _____ of a great adversary.
    A. Jaws
    B. Scalp
    C. Spine

15. Describe Teebo's headdress.

16. Identify the Ewok who fought beside the Rebels when they attacked the guarded bunker containing the Death Star's shield generator.

17. Which Ewok made an impassioned case to have the Rebels released from tribal captivity and spared Logray's sacrificial ceremony?

18. Who tricked the Ewoks into freeing the Rebels?

JEDI MASTER BONUS #3

Name the Ewok who smoked a pipe.

---

19. Who did the Ewoks consider a "golden god"?

20. Which Ewok was responsible for maintaining the ancient traditions and rituals of the tribe?
    A. Chief Chirpa
    B. Logray
    C. Paploo

21. Who dramatically told the story of the Galactic Empire and its evil tyranny throughout the galaxy?

22. Identify the Ewok who convinced the village elders to make the Rebels honorary members of the tribe.

REBEL RUMBLINGS & IMPERIAL TRANSMISSIONS
Star Wars: A New Hope

As part of your training to be a Jedi Knight, you must decipher the following intercepted Rebel and Imperial transmissions by either determining the actual identity of the person speaking or providing the complete dialogue.

---

1. What was Darth Vader's reply when Grand Moff Tarkin suggested that Obi-Wan Kenobi "surely must be dead by now"?
   A. "Nevertheless, I feel a tremor in the Force."
   B. "Don't underestimate the power of the Force."
   C. "Obi-Wan is here! I can feel his presence."

2. (Fill in the Blank) Aboard the Death Star battle station, Tarkin warned Princess Leia, "You're far too trusting. _____ is too remote to make an effective demonstration. But don't worry. We will deal with your Rebel friends soon enough."

3. (Fill in the Blank) After an explosion rocked the Rebel Blockade Runner, C-3PO asked R2-D2, "Did you hear that? They've shut down the main _____. We'll be destroyed for sure. This is madness!"

4. Who made the comment that a lightsaber was "not as clumsy or as random as a blaster"?

    A. Luke Skywalker
    B. Obi-Wan Kenobi
    C. Darth Vader

5. What was Luke's response at the Mos Eisley spaceport when an Imperial stormtrooper asked him how long he had owned the droids C-3PO and R2-D2?
    A. "Two or three harvests"
    B. "Longer than I care to remember"
    C. "About three or four seasons"

6. (True or False) When a Jawa ran up to his landspeeder and began fondling it, Luke complained, "I can't abide these Jawas. Disgusting creatures."

JEDI MASTER BONUS #1

Who said, "You can't win. But there are alternatives to fighting"?

---

7. (Fill in the Blank) Darth Vader admonished Princess Leia, "Don't play games with me, Your Highness. You weren't on any mercy mission this time. You passed directly through a _____ system. Several transmissions were beamed to this ship by Rebel spies."

8. Who called R2-D2 an "overweight glob of grease"?

9. Who referred to Tatooine as the farthest planet from the "bright center of the universe"?
    A. Ben Kenobi
    B. C-3PO
    C. Luke Skywalker

10. Who described the Force as "a lot of simple tricks and nonsense"?

11. (Fill in the Blank) When Grand Moff Tarkin complained that Princess Leia had lied to him about the whereabouts of the Rebel base, Vader calmly replied, "I told you she would never _____ betray the Rebellion."

12. (Fill in the blank with the correct number) After realizing that Alderaan had been totally obliterated, a stunned Han Solo commented, "The entire starfleet couldn't destroy the whole planet. It'd take a _____ ships with more firepower than I've . . ."

JEDI MASTER BONUS #2

When it was painfully obvious that the Death Star had captured the *Millennium Falcon* in a tractor beam, who instructed Chewie to reverse the freighter ship and "lock in the auxiliary power"?

---

13. (Fill in the Blank) When Darth Vader and Obi-Wan Kenobi confronted one another aboard the Death Star, the Dark Knight told his former teacher, "We meet again, at last. The _____ is now complete."

14. (Fill in the Blank) Han Solo acknowledged his mercenary intentions when he confessed to Leia, "I ain't in this for your _____, and I'm not in it for you, Princess. I expect to be well paid. I'm in it for the money!"

15. Who greeted Leia at the Yavin Rebel base with a heartfelt embrace and the words of relief, "You're safe! We had feared the worst. When we heard about Alderaan, we were afraid that you were . . . lost along with your father"?
    A. Commander Willard
    B. General Dodonna
    C. Commander Narra

16. Who prematurely boasted, "This will be a day long remembered. It has seen the end of Kenobi and it will soon see the end of the Rebellion"?

17. Who considered the Rebel attack against the Death Star battle station an act of "suicide" rather than "courage"?
    A. Grand Moff Tarkin
    B. C-3PO
    C. Han Solo

18. As the Rebel attack squadron prepared for the Battle of Yavin, who asked, "You wouldn't want my life to get boring, would you?"
    A. Han Solo
    B. C-3PO
    C. Luke Skywalker

JEDI MASTER BONUS #3

During the assault on the Death Star, who instructed Luke to "blow this thing and go home"?

---

19. (Fill in the Blank) Luke Skywalker complained to C-3PO that he wished the droid could "alter time, speed up the _____, or teleport" the boy off Tatooine.

20. Who observed that Luke was "not a farmer . . . He has too much of his father in him"?

21. Who described R2-D2 as "faulty" and "malfunctioning"?

22. (Fill in the Blank) After Luke referred to the *Millennium Falcon* as "a piece of junk," Han Solo shot back defensively, "She may not look like much, but she's got it where it counts, kid. I've added some special _____ myself."

23. Who menacingly said to Princess Leia, "Before your execution I would like you to be my guest at a ceremony that will make this battle station operational"?

24. Identify the character who classified the Imperials as "slugs."
    A. Princess Leia
    B. Han Solo
    C. Chewie

JEDI MASTER BONUS #4

(Fill in the blank with the correct number)

When Jabba the Hutt and his alien pirates confronted Han Solo in the docking bay at the Mos Eisley spaceport, the crime lord offered the Corellian smuggler a deal, with a warning attached, of course: ". . . for an extra, say _____ percent, I'll give you a little more time . . . but this is it. If you disappoint me again, I'll put a price on your head so large you won't be able to go near a civilized system for the rest of your short life."

---

25. Who uttered the galactic pearl of prudence, "It's not wise to upset a Wookiee"?

26. (True or False) A skeptical Han Solo referred to the Force and lightsabers as "hokey religions and ancient weapons."

27. Who demanded that Princess Leia be "terminated . . . immediately"?

28. (Fill in the Blank) After Luke acknowledged that with the Force's guidance he "could almost see the remote," Kenobi congratulated his new pupil, "That's good. You have taken your first step into a _____ world."

29. (Fill in the Blank) After the *Millennium Falcon* was captured by the Death Star's tractor beam, an Imperial officer reported to Darth Vader, "There's no one on board, sir. According to the log, the crew abandoned ship right after takeoff. It must be a _____, sir. Several of the escape pods have been jettisoned."

30. Identify the character who asked, "Who's the more foolish . . . the fool or the fool who follows him?"
    A. Ben Kenobi
    B. Princess Leia
    C. Luke Skywalker

31. (Fill in the Blank) After Luke complained that it was a "wonder that the whole station" didn't know they were aboard the Death Star, Han snapped back, "Bring them on! I prefer a _____ fight to all this sneaking around."

32. Who informed Kenobi that a "power loss at one of the terminals" would allow the *Millennium Falcon* to flee the Death Star?

33. Who told Luke and Han that Princess Leia was "scheduled to be terminated"?

34. (Fill in the Blank) "Your _____ lies along a different path than mine," Kenobi conceded to Luke. "The Force will be with you . . . always!"

35. Who asked, "Aren't you a little short to be a stormtrooper?"

36. (Fill in the Blank) Darth Vader described Obi-Wan Kenobi's presence aboard the Death Star as a "_____ in the Force."

JEDI MASTER BONUS #5

(Fill in the Blank)

After Darth Vader informed Tarkin that he could sense his old master's presence, the Imperial Grand Moff skeptically replied, "The Jedi are extinct, their _____ has gone out of the universe."

JEDI MASTER BONUS #6

Which character was referred to as "all that was left" of the Jedi "religion"?

---

37. Who was supposed to be "the brains" behind Princess Leia's rescue from the Death Star battle station?
    A. Ben Kenobi
    B. Luke Skywalker
    C. Han Solo

38. Which two characters said at different times, "I've got a bad feeling about this"?

39. Who described Chewie as "a big walking carpet"?

40. Who called Darth Vader "a master of evil"?

41. Owen Lars referred to Kenobi as a "crazy old wizard" and Darth Vader called him an "old man." Who disparagingly suggested that the former Jedi Knight was nothing more than a "fossil" that had been dug up on Tatooine?

42. (Fill in the Blank) As Imperial stormtroopers fired on the escaping *Millennium Falcon*, Han Solo wished aloud, "I hope the

old man got that tractor beam out of _____, or this is going to be a real short trip."

JEDI MASTER BONUS #7

Who screamed, "We've lost lateral controls!" as TIE fighters subjected the fleeing *Millennium Falcon* to a barrage of firepower?

---

43. Who demanded that Obi-Wan Kenobi "not be allowed to escape" from the Death Star battle station?

44. (Fill in the Blank) Leia angrily denounced Han Solo to Luke Skywalker when they arrived at the Yavin base: "Your friend is quite a _____. I wonder if he really cares about anything . . . or anyone."

45. Who said about Han, "He's got to follow his own path. No one can choose it for him"?

46. (Fill in the Blank) When an explosion hit near the droids aboard Princess Leia's Blockade Runner, C-3PO complained, "I should have known better than to trust the _____ of a half-sized thermocapsulary dehousing assister."

47. Who accused Leia of being "part of the Rebel Alliance" and of being a "traitor"?

48. Identify the Imperial officer who warned, "Until this battle station is fully operational we are vulnerable. The Rebel Alliance is too well equipped. They're more dangerous than you realize."
    A. Admiral Motti
    B. General Tagge
    C. Grand Moff Tarkin

JEDI MASTER BONUS #8

(Fill in the Blanks)

Princess Leia stored a holographic message to Obi-Wan Kenobi in R2-D2's memory banks, which said, "General Kenobi, years ago you _____ my father in the Clone Wars. Now he begs you to help him in his _____ against the Empire. I regret that I am unable to present my father's request to you in person; but my ship has fallen under attack, and I'm afraid my _____ to bring you to Alderaan has failed. I have placed information vital to the _____ of the Rebellion into the memory systems of this R2-D2 unit. My father will know how to retrieve it. You must see this droid safely delivered to him on Alderaan. This is our most _____ hour. Help me, Obi-Wan Kenobi, you're my only hope."

49. Who said, "There'll be no escape for the Princess this time"?
    A. Grand Moff Tarkin
    B. Darth Vader
    C. C-3PO

50. (Fill in the Blank) As the *Tantive IV* escape pod rotated through space en route to Tatooine, C-3PO observed, "That's funny, the _____ doesn't look as bad from out here."

51. Who asked, "Will this ever end?"

52. (Fill in the blank with the characters' names) When Luke's uncle Owen requested that the boy stay on the Tatooine moisture farm for "one more season" instead of going to the Academy, Luke shot back, "Yeah, that's what you said last year when _____ and _____ left."

53. (Fill in the Blank) Darth Vader lectured Admiral Motti, "Don't be too proud of this technological _____ you've constructed. The ability to destroy a planet is insignificant next to the power of the Force."

54. (True or False) When Han Solo asked Ben Kenobi if he was involved in "some kind of local trouble," the old Jedi Knight replied rather evasively, "Let's just say we'd like to avoid any Imperial entanglements."

JEDI MASTER BONUS #9

(Fill in the Blanks)

Admiral Motti told Darth Vader in a sarcastic tone aboard the Death Star, "Don't try to frighten us with your _____ ways, Lord Vader. Your sad devotion to that ancient religion has not helped you conjure up the stolen tapes, or given you _____ enough to find the Rebel's hidden fort . . ."

---

55. Who boasted of the Death Star's awesome firepower, "Any attack made by the Rebels against this station would be a useless gesture, no matter what technical data they've obtained. This station is now the ultimate power in the universe. I suggest we use it"?
    A. Admiral Motti
    B. General Tagge
    C. Grand Moff Tarkin

56. (Fill in the Blank) Ben Kenobi described Luke Skywalker's father as "the best starpilot in the galaxy, and a _____ warrior."
    A. Skilled
    B. Cunning
    C. Natural

57. (Fill in the Blank) As the droids clumsily worked their way across the desert wasteland of Tatooine, C-3PO complained to R2-D2, "I've got to rest before I fall apart. My _____ are almost frozen."

58. Identify the Imperial officer who bragged that the Empire would "crush the Rebellion with one swift stroke"?

59. Who found Admiral Motti's "lack of faith disturbing"?

60. Name the Imperial who described Princess Leia's "resistance to the mind probe" as "considerable"?

JEDI MASTER BONUS #10

Who referred to Han Solo as "the best smuggler in the business"?

---

61. (Fill in the Blank) While fleeing Imperial cruisers aboard the *Millennium Falcon,* Han Solo took the time to lecture Luke Skywalker: "Traveling through hyperspace isn't like dusting crops, boy! Without precise calculations we could fly right through a star or bounce too close to a _____ and that'd end your trip real quick . . ."?

62. (Fill in the Blank) After the Death Star annihilated Alderaan, Ben Kenobi acknowledged that he "felt a great disturbance in the Force . . . as if millions of voices suddenly cried out in _____ and were suddenly silenced."

63. (True or False) C-3PO insisted to Luke Skywalker that he was an "excellent translator" and "very good at telling stories."

64. Identify the Imperial officer who confessed that if the Rebels had obtained a complete technical readout of the Death Star,

then it was possible, "however unlikely, that they might find a weakness and exploit it"?

65. (Fill in the Blank) In teaching Luke Skywalker the ways of the Force, Kenobi instructed his young student to "let go your _____ self and act on instinct."

66. Which Imperial bragged, "There'll be no one to stop us this time"?
    A. Grand Moff Tarkin
    B. Admiral Motti
    C. Darth Vader

67. Who said, "You know that little droid is going to cause me a lot of trouble"?
    A. C-3PO
    B. Luke Skywalker
    C. Han Solo

68. (True or False) When Grand Moff Tarkin announced that the Emperor had dissolved the Imperial Senate, he proclaimed that "fear will keep the local systems in line" in absence of the bureaucracy.

JEDI MASTER BONUS #11

During the Rebel assault on the Death Star, which fighter pilot complimented Wedge Antilles on his "good shooting"?

THE NITPICKER'S GUIDE:
Star Wars: A New Hope

We have reviewed the first installment of the Star Wars *trilogy over and over again—scene by scene, and often frame by frame. It's truly amazing the number of bloopers, snafus, inconsistencies, impossibilities and just plain screwups the movie contains when you look hard enough. We would like to make it clear, though, that we are in no way finding fault with this film classic. We are still avid fans and would defend* Star Wars *to the far ends of the galaxy, but we're not unobservant. Besides, watching for bloopers is a lot of fun!*

A Sudden Case of Laryngitis

When our heroes are in the Death Star's trash compactor, watch Luke's mouth just after you hear the dianoga roar. As he turns his head around, you can actually see him mouth the words, "What was that?" but nothing comes out. You'll have to watch closely, though, because it's hardly noticeable.

Mirror, Mirror

Another blooper that occurs several times in the movie is a reversed or "flipped" image created during postproduction editing. This happens when an image is "flipped" as the film is being pieced together, thus making it appear backward. One scene in particular is when Darth Vader and Ben Kenobi are engaged in their lightsaber duel aboard the Death Star. Look closely at

Vader's life system computer just below his breastplate while he says, "You should not have come back." It's backward! (Note: In actuality, the entire scene is "flipped," but the life system computer is easier to detect.)

Danger: Low Clearance

One of the more infamous blooper scenes also occurs on the Death Star. When the stormtroopers blast their way into the Control Room where C-3PO and R2-D2 are hiding, the Imperial soldier on the far right knocks his head against the "not fully raised" automatic door.

Peekaboo, I See You

When R2-D2 is initially placed into the sandcrawler by the Jawa traders, he looks around at all the other creatures inside the desert transport vehicle. We see another astromech droid, R5-D4, followed by a camera shot of more creatures, and then another view of R5-D4. Immediately following the second shot, the camera turns back to R2-D2 and you can see Kenny Baker's face through the little droid's domed head.

Have Blaster, Will Travel

At the beginning of the scene in which Darth Vader interrogates a Rebel aboard the *Tantive IV*, the leftmost stormtrooper is holding his blaster at waist level. When the camera cuts to another angle, the Imperial soldier is holding the weapon up to his chest. But when the camera returns to the original angle, the blaster does a David Copperfield and is back at the stormtrooper's waist.

C-3PO Shows How You Can Get Those Nasty Stains Out

As C-3PO walks past the skeleton of the dragonlike creature on Tatooine, the droid has a large grease stain down the left side of his golden chest. A few scenes later, the stain appears on his right side. Once again, this is a direct result of "flipping" an image in postproduction editing.

If It Ain't Broke, Don't Fix It

After Luke's uncle Owen purchases the R5-D4 astromech droid from the Jawas, it malfunctions. As Owen gestures to R2-D2 and the little droid's head turns, the audience sees the previous shot of the diminutive desert traders prepping R5-D4 from BEFORE Owen Lars decided to buy him.

Just Like One of those <u>Bad</u> Japanese Martial Arts Movies

In all the scenes involving Luke's aunt Beru, her lips are never moving in synch with her spoken dialogue. After the film's original release, George Lucas reportedly felt that the actress's voice was too low and dubbed over all of her lines in succeeding prints of the movie.

Sleight of Hand

During the dinner scene between Luke and his aunt and uncle, the boy is holding a cup in his left hand. A few frames later, he is holding it in his right hand, which is most likely a result of the images being "flipped."

Maybe Luke Should Have Thrown the Circuit Breaker

In Ben Kenobi's small hut on Tatooine's Western Dune Sea, the old Jedi Knight is telling Luke of his father when C-3PO requests that he be powered off. Although Luke complies, the droid's head turns in reaction to Ben's energizing of Anakin Skywalker's lightsaber.

Where's a Crash Test Dummy When You Need One?

If you freeze the frames immediately before Han Solo blasts the Rodian bounty hunter, Greedo, in the Mos Eisley cantina, it is obvious that a *really* bad-looking dummy is substituted for the actor prior to Greedo's death from the weapon's blast. The stunt dummy is much taller and thinner than the actor, is wearing a different jacket, and worse still—is not pointing a gun at Han!

Maybe Greedo Was Wearing a Blasterproof Vest

While Luke, Ben and the two droids head to the Mos Eisley docking bay to board the *Millennium Falcon*, the camera cuts to an Imperial spy—a hooded alien with huge, round eyes and an elongated snout. As he watches our heroes from the shadows, a variety of humanoids and alien creatures pass by to and fro in the background. One in particular bears an uncanny resemblance to Jabba the Hutt's hired muscle, Greedo, whom Han killed with a blaster only a few moments earlier. Of course, it is possible that the alien is just another member of the Rodian species, but would he be wearing the same clothing as Greedo? Yeah, that's what we thought, too.

Hey, Buddy, You Better Take a Taxi Home

Just after Han tells Luke and Ben, "It looks like someone's beginning to take an interest in your handiwork," the camera pans over the crowded Mos Eisley cantina to a pair of Imperial stormtroopers walking toward their corner table. Pay close attention to the mousy-looking alien with the see-through eyes. As he takes a drink, he very distinctly misses his mouth and hits his chin instead.

Hey, Which Way Did He Go?

In the scene where Han and Chewie run into the cockpit of the *Falcon* during the shoot-'em-up with the Imperial stormtroopers in the Mos Eisley docking bay, there is a person with a green shirt standing in the corridor. A moment later, he moves out of the shot. (Note: This blooper only appears in the letterbox version of the movie.)

Bouncing Off the Walls

During the opening sequence of the movie aboard the Rebel Blockade Runner, Princess Leia is seen storing the Death Star's technical readouts into R2-D2's memory banks to be retrieved by Obi-Wan Kenobi. After she completes her mission, the little droid starts to roll away. However, if the scene had continued, R2-D2 would have rolled into the wall of the transport.

But Can You Saw a Woman in Half?

Near the end of the segment in which R2-D2 projects to Luke the Princess Leia hologram, C-3PO is shown holding a rag. In the next camera shot he isn't, in the succeeding shot ("I'm sorry, sir, but he appears to have picked up a slight flutter") he has the rag again, and in the final shot the droid is shown empty-handed once more.

Is This Where Eveready® Got the Idea for the Darth Vader/Energizer® Bunny Commercial?

During the infamous lightsaber duel between Obi-Wan Kenobi and Darth Vader aboard the Death Star, there are several times when you can see a white power cord used to illuminate Kenobi's Jedi weapon.

Only the Shadow Knows

How can power swords, which project narrow beams of meter-long pure energy, cast shadows? They can be noticed in several instances on the corridor walls during the Kenobi-Vader lightsaber battle.

He'll Never Get a Job Colorizing Movies for Ted Turner

Just after Vader kills Obi-Wan, the Dark Lord's lightsaber blade is white instead of the usual red. Coloring of the weapons' beams was added in postproduction, but reportedly an optical effects technician didn't take care of business in this particular scene.

Now You See It, Now You Don't

There is a medium-brown macrame-type "shawl" hanging on the left side of the plaster arch in Obi-Wan's house. Right after Kenobi says to Luke, "This is the weapon of a Jedi Knight . . . ," the shawl disappears from the scene. But after Luke turns off the lightsaber, it shows back up for a return engagement.

And We Thought Michael Jackson was "The Gloved One"

When Luke is sitting at the bar in the Mos Eisley saloon, he takes a quick glance around the room. The camera then gives us shots of various alien creatures, including two blue-skinned Duros engaged in lively conversation. If you look at their hands, the one on the right has immense, purple, and *very* alien-looking fingers and palms, but the Duros on the left (remember the two are of the same species) is wearing white gloves over obviously human hands.

Excuse Me, Lord Vader, But Did You Say Something?

During a scene between Vader and Grand Moff Tarkin aboard the Death Star, the Dark Lord stops talking but keeps gesturing as though he is continuing to speak dialogue. Tarkin doesn't reply until after Vader is finished with his gesticulation. It is painfully obvious with this particular sequence that there existed some difficulty in synchronizing James Earl Jones' voice with David Prowse's movements.

"Chewie, Reverse Engines While We've Got a Chance!"

When the *Millennium Falcon* is captured by the Death Star's tractor beam, it is pulled aboard the Imperial battle station. As the stock freighter enters the hangar bay, watch the bottom center of the ship as it passes through the massive portal. The edge of the door is illuminated with a white light, but as the *Falcon* passes through, the light is "broken" by the vertical pole that was used to hold the visual effects model of the ship.

One Step Forward, Two Steps Back

During the firefight inside the Death Star's detention area, Leia shoots a hole in the grate leading to the trash compactor and jumps in, tossing her blaster to Luke. Chewie begins to follow and places one hairy foot into the hole. The camera then cuts away to Han firing his gun down the corridor of the battle station. The camera cuts back to the Wookie, who once again walks toward the hole leading to the compactor and places the same foot into the grate opening. For some unknown reason, Chewie enters the trash compactor twice.

Wonder Woman

Watch Leia's left hand as she grabs a metal pole in the trash compactor to try and brace the walls. The rod actually crunches momentarily when she grasps it, and when she loosens her grip it returns to normal. .

A Change of Plans

During the Rebel briefing by General Dodonna, he shows the starfighter pilots the Death Star's technical readouts downloaded from R2-D2's memory banks. The detailed plans are flawed, however, because they show the main turret centered along the equator of the moon-shaped battle station. As demonstrated during the film's climactic Rebel assault, the Death Star's turret was clearly on the northern hemisphere.

He Talks Out of Both Sides of His Mouth

As the Rebel fleet of starfighters approaches the Death Star, Red Leader's helmet-attached microphone switches from side to side; it's particularly noticeable as he speaks the line, "All wings, report in!"

After Red Leader says "Watch it, there's a lot of fire coming from the right side of that deflection tower," you can't help but notice that Luke's microphone switches over to the opposite side of his helmet for that camera shot.

And We Thought the Death Star Was Fully Operational

During any scene set in the battle station's conference room you can see the stage panels incessantly swinging back and forth in the background behind Grand Moff Tarkin and Darth Vader. This is especially noticeable during the sequence just after the *Millennium Falcon* is brought aboard the Death Star by a tractor beam. As an Imperial comlink voice briefs Tarkin and Vader on the capture of the freighter, a vertical bracelike beam between the two sways from left to right like a pendulum.

No Strain to See the Crane

As Princess Leia is about to be tortured aboard the Death Star, you can plainly see the crane in Leia's cell that was used to make the interrogation droid appear to float. It's between the robot and the right edge of the door.

On a Clear Day You Can See Forever

When Luke and Ben enter the Mos Eisley cantina the camera pans around the galactic watering hole, showing us a virtual rogue's gallery of alien thieves and smugglers. One exotic-looking life-form in particular is a small, "mousy" alien who is begging for a drink at the bar (he's the same one who hit his chin with a drink). Look closely at his eyes as he turns his head and you can see right through his head.

I Thought You Said This Ship Came Fully Loaded?

When Chewie escorts Luke, Ben and the two droids to the Mos Eisley docking bay, the audience gets its first glimpse of the *Millennium Falcon.* Take note of the top right of the screen: the freighter is missing its trademark radar dish.

It Depends If You Are Inside Looking Out, Or Outside Looking In

If you look at the TIE starfighters closely during the Rebel assault on the Death Star, you will notice a distinct difference in configuration of the cockpit windows of the miniature models compared to the pilot's view from inside of the Imperial fighters.

Depending on whether the camera is providing an interior shot from within the cockpit or an exterior shot of the visual effects model, there is also an inconsistency in the number of window frames on the *Millennium Falcon.*

Since When Did Laser Rifles Eject Spent Cases?

The movie's laser rifles were in reality modified Sterling 9mm submachine guns. When filming the *Star Wars'* multitude of firefights and shoot-outs, blank bullets were utilized to simulate "kickbacks" and to let the cast member or extra know when the rifle was fired. Unfortunately, the altered weapons ejected spent cases as if they were real bullets.

They Must Have Still Been Firing Blanks

Just after Han shoots the control panel inside the Death Star and yells to Luke, take a close look over his shoulder on the screen's left side. Its kind of hard to NOT notice the two racks of security cameras hanging from the ceiling, undamaged, even after our heroes very painstakingly destroyed them all.

Maybe She Didn't Like the Smell on That Side of the Compactor

After Luke gets pulled under a sea of waste by the dianoga, Leia and Han wait nervously for him to resurface. The camera cuts to the princess as she leans to screen left against some garbage. The camera then goes in for a close-up of Leia, who is now leaning forward and to screen right with no time to change positions between camera shots.

Only the Shadow Knows . . . Again

Right before the line "Didn't we just leave this party?" when Han and Chewie arrive in the corridor leading to the *Millennium Falcon* ahead of Luke and Leia, you can see the shadows of the latter two as they await their cue to run in.

More Flip-Flops Than a Politician

After Leia speaks the line of dialogue, "We have no time for sorrows, Commander," the camera cuts to R2-D2 being unloaded from a transport that has just arrived at the Yavin Rebel base. The scene was obviously reversed during postproduction editing. The most obvious tell-tale sign: Han's holster is hanging off his left hip instead of the usual right.

Maybe They Need to Get the Speedometer Recalibrated

After the *Millennium Falcon* escapes from the Death Star and battles free of the Imperial TIE starfighters, the freighter makes the jump to hyperspace. The camera cuts back to a conversation between Grand Moff Tarkin and Darth Vader, and then back again to the cockpit of the *Falcon*. As Han and Leia talk away, the plain stars of "normal space" and not the blurry, elongated stars of hyperspace, are clearly visible outside the windows.

Hit and Run

Near the beginning of the movie, C-3PO dents the left side of his head when he falls and breaks off one of his arms. The dent remains on the droid all through the film, but in one particular shot at the end, when he's standing next to Princess Leia in the Rebel Control Room, the dent is on his right side and Leia is on his other side, due to the scene's postproduction "flip."

He Talks Out of Both Sides of His Mouth . . . Again

After Biggs Darklighter's death, when Luke's starfighter is fired upon by Imperial forces, the boy speaks into his microphone announcing to the Control Room that he's all right. The audience gets a view of one of the controllers, whose headset is on his left ear, but in the next camera cut it's on his right.

Princess Carrie?

In the scene right after the Death Star is destroyed, Luke arrives at the Yavin Rebel base and is reunited with Han and Leia. The princess comes running up to him just as he descends the X-wing's ladder, but he calls the character by the actress's name, as he joyfully yells, "Carrie!" (Note: Although some fans swear that they hear "Hey!"—ourselves included—or some other words to that effect, George Lucas has admitted that Mark Hamill inadvertently called out, "Carrie!" during filming of the scene.)

Keep Smiling, Princess

During the medals ceremony after the Death Star's destruction, we are shown a close-up of Han, and then the camera cuts back to Princess Leia, who is displaying a very wide smile. She turns to screen right to get Solo's Hero of Yavin medallion from General Dodonna, but when the camera shows us a slightly wider angle, Leia's mouth is closed.

The Eyes Have It

George Lucas wanted to make the eyes of Darth Vader's mask completely dark, but was unable to achieve the effect in the first film. Although it was fixed in the other two installments of the *Star Wars* saga, you can actually see the face of David Prowse, "the man behind the mask," through the eyeholes.

Chewie, Will You Please Stand Still?

Watch the Wookie when the walls of the Death Star's trash compactor begin closing in on our heroes. His position changes in three camera cuts: first, he is shown pushing against the wall with his hairy hands; second, he turns to screen right to grab his crossbow laser; finally, we are shown a shot of Chewie once again holding the wall.

Watch That Last Step, C-3PO!

During the scene on Tatooine, when Luke is cleaning R2-D2 (and just after the line of dialogue, "Well, my little friend, you've got something jammed in here real good . . .") the hologram of Princess Leia is projected, and C-3PO falls off the step he is on.

Perhaps It's Like a Soap Opera: Unless You See a Dead Body—They Aren't dead

As the Rebel starfighters attack the Death Star, Porkins (Red 6) is killed during the conflict. Later on in the movie, as Luke is piloting his X-wing down a trench in the battle station, Darth Vader secures a direct hit on a section of the boy's fighter. He asks R2-D2 to determine if he can repair the damage, and immediately following the scene, someone queries on the intercom, ". . . Red 6, have you seen Red 5?" But how could Red 6 answer? He's dead already!

STAR WARFARE

The civil war between the Alliance to Restore the Republic and the tyrannical Galactic Empire involved a vast war machine on both sides. From a starfighter's pivoting blaster cannons to a Jedi Knight's lightsaber, test your knowledge of Rebel and Imperial weaponry.

---

1. What type of tactical weapons did the Rebel fighters use to penetrate the defenses of both Death Star battle stations?
   A. Ion cannons
   B. Proton torpedoes
   C. Laser cannons

2. (True or False) Planetary ion cannons were used to protect Rebel transports evacuating the Rebel base on Hoth from orbital assault by Imperial forces.

3. Identify the specialized equipment aboard starfighters and other military vessels that worked in conjunction with the ships' navicomputers to calculate hostile targets' trajectories and attack and intercept courses.

4. (Fill in the Blank) Princess Leia, in the disguise of a bounty hunter, tried to impress Jabba the Hutt by threatening to blow up the crime lord and his palace on Tatooine with a _____ detonator.

5. How many forward laser cannons were mounted on a Rebel Y-wing model starfighter?

6. What was the armament complement of wing-tipped laser cannons on an X-wing starfighter?

JEDI MASTER BONUS #1

How many quad laser cannons and concussion missile launchers were installed on the *Millennium Falcon?*

---

7. How many pivoting blaster cannons were mounted on the wings of a Rebel A-wing starfighter?

8. (Fill in the Blank) An Imperial AT-AT's armament consisted of heavy _____ cannons mounted on each side of the walker's movable "head" and under the "chin."
    A. ion
    B. laser
    C. blaster

9. What type of crossbow laser was the Wookiee Chewbacca's weapon of choice?

10. What was the color of Darth Vader's lightsaber blade?
     A. Red
     B. Blue
     C. Yellow

11. What type of weapons were in the knees of Boba Fett's Mandalore battle armor?
     A. Lasers
     B. Rocket darts
     C. Sonic stunners

12. (Fill in the blanks with the correct numbers) B-wing starfighters were armed with _____ internally mounted proton torpedo launchers and _____ small blaster cannons.

JEDI MASTER BONUS #2

Where was the forward gun pod hidden on the *Millennium Falcon?*

---

13. Identify the traditional double-edged, axelike weapon favored by Tusken Raiders.
   A. Faderggii
   B. Gaderffii
   C. Gallandro

14. What type of weapon neutralized a ship by firing bursts of energy that overloaded and fused the circuitry of a target's mechanical and computer systems?

15. (Fill in the Blank) The *Millennium Falcon* was armed with a _____ light laser cannon.

16. What was the thermoformed substance used in the construction of many forms of battle armor?
   A. Plasticized tritanium
   B. Tripolymer composite
   C. Plastoid

17. (True or False) Proton torpedoes could be fired from specialized shoulder- or back-mounted delivery system launchers.

18. Military speeder bikes, like those used by Imperial scout troopers, were armed with what type of weapons?
   A. Blaster cannons
   B. Laser cannons
   C. Ion cannons

JEDI MASTER BONUS #3

What type of weapon's discharge emitted a smell similar to ozone?

---

19. (True or False) An Imperial scout walker's armament included a concussion grenade launcher.

20. (Fill in the Blank) A Rebel B-wing starfighter's primary and secondary wingtips featured ion cannons, while the command pod housed a mounted _____ cannon.

21. What was another name for the parcels of concentrated light energy fired from blasters?
    A. Bolts
    B. Strokes
    C. Arrays

22. What type of sublight-speed projectiles made up part of a Rebel starfighter's armament?

23. (Fill in the Blank) Manifold turbolaser-gun and ion-cannon artillery installations were often referred to as _____ batteries.

24. Where was the antipersonnel blaster aimed and fired from in certain starfighters and transport ships such as the *Millennium Falcon?*
    A. Copilot's station
    B. Gunner's station
    C. Pilot's station

> **JEDI MASTER BONUS #4**
>
> How many turbolaser batteries were part of the armament complement of Admiral Ackbar's personal flagship, *Home One?*

25. How many meters in length was the blade or narrow beam of light produced by a lightsaber?
    A. One
    B. One-and-a-half
    C. Two

26. Where were the quad laser cannons located on the *Millennium Falcon?*

27. How many proton torpedo launchers were featured on bounty hunter Boba Fett's starfighter, *Slave I?*
    A. One
    B. Two
    C. Four

28. (True or False) Even complete particle shielding force fields could not entirely deflect proton-scattering torpedoes.

29. (Fill in the Blank) Bowcasters fired energy bullets called _____, which exploded upon impact.

30. (True or False) Usually a training tool, a seeker could be reprogrammed to fire high-powered, lethal blaster bolts at specific targets.

31. (Fill in the Blank) Snowspeeders on Hoth employed two forward heavy laser cannons and rear-mounted _____ cannons.

JEDI MASTER BONUS #5

How many thousands of turbolaser battery emplacements dappled the canyonlike surface of the original Death Star?

---

32. (True or False) Imperial Star Destroyers utilized turbolasers and ion cannon batteries as part of their massive arsenal of offensive weaponry.

33. What was the shape of thermal detonators?

34. What caused a thermal detonator to explode once it was activated?
    A. Negatively charged antiprotons
    B. Controlled annihilation of matter and antimatter
    C. Fusion reaction

35. How many laser cannons were used in the armament of Imperial TIE fighters?
    A. Two
    B. Four
    C. Six

36. (Fill in the Blank) Turbolasers required constant adjustment of temperatures from built-in _____ cooling systems.

37. (True or False) The blasts from concussion missiles could penetrate and obliterate even heavily armored targets.

JEDI MASTER BONUS #6

What was another name for the energy cells that provided the power to operate blasters and lightsabers?

---

38. (Fill in the Blank) Armed for star warfare, the Mon-Calamari-designed starship, *Home One,* had thirty-six _____ cannon emplacements.

39. What was the more common name for the Sand People's deadly gaderffii weapon?

40. (True or False) Planetary ion cannons were mounted in multistory, hexagonal free-standing towers that utilized their own power sources.

41. (True or False) As part of the intense Jedi Knighthood training, years of tradition decreed that lightsabers be constructed by their owners.

42. (True or False) Turbolasers discharged hotter and more focused energy bolts than regular laser cannons.

43. (Fill in the Blank) Rebel Y-wing starfighters were armed with rear-mounted _____ ion cannons.

JEDI MASTER BONUS #7

In addition to its powerful, planet-destroying superlaser, how many turbolaser batteries were part of the armament complement of the second Imperial Death Star?

PRINCESS BY VIRTUE, REBEL BY CHOICE: LEIA ORGANA
Imperial Security Bureau (ISB) Dossier #22530-077

1. Who was Leia's foster father?

2. What title did he hold in the Royal Family of Alderaan?
    A. Duke
    B. Viceroy
    C. Prince

3. During what terrible conflict did Leia's father fight side-by-side with his comrade Obi-Wan Kenobi?

4. Which distinctive legislative position did Leia hold in the Imperial Senate prior to its dissolution by the Emperor?
    A. Speaker of the Congress
    B. Majority leader of the Senatorial Cabinet
    C. Youngest member of the Senate

5. (True or False) While Leia fought for legislative reforms on the Senate floor, she led a dangerous double life as a major undercover operative for the Alliance to Restore the Republic.

6. On which planet did Leia receive word that Rebel spies had obtained the technical plans to the Emperor's new weapon— a battle station the size of a small moon?
    A. Ralltiir
    B. Mimban
    C. Beto II

JEDI MASTER BONUS #1

What was the number of Leia's detention *cell* during her imprisonment aboard the original Death Star?

---

7. Why did Darth Vader keep Leia's capture aboard the Rebel Blockade Runner *Tantive IV* a secret?

8. What order did Vader give Imperial troops that ensured her apprehension would remain secret?

9. Which planet was Leia's destination before her consular ship was intercepted by Vader's Imperial Star Destroyer?
    A. Alderaan
    B. Tatooine
    C. Yavin

10. What type of mission did Leia insist the *Tantive IV* was on?

11. As a prisoner of Darth Vader and Grand Moff Tarkin, Leia underwent excruciating torture as the Imperials sought to discover not only the location of the Death Star's stolen technical plans, but also the whereabouts of the main Rebel base. Identify one of the torturous methods used by Vader and Moff in an effort to force information from the princess.
    A. Mind probe
    B. Neurosomatic technique
    C. Neural metaphasic shock

12. In an attempt to save her beloved homeworld, Alderaan, from destruction by the Death Star, on what remote planet did Leia say the base of operations for the Rebel Alliance was located?

JEDI MASTER BONUS #2

How many stormtroopers captured Princess Leia aboard the Blockade Runner?

JEDI MASTER BONUS #3

What was Leia's signet of office?

---

13. How did Leia first appear to Luke Skywalker?

14. What was Leia's two-word response after Luke informed her aboard the Death Star, "I'm Luke Skywalker. I'm here to rescue you"?
    A. "Aren't you a little short to be a stormtrooper?"
    B. "You're who?"
    C. "Do you have a plan or are you making this up as you go along?"

15. What color was the long, elegant dress Princess Leia wore during the medallion awards ceremony for the Heroes of Yavin?

16. (True or False) Leia insulted Han Solo just prior to the Battle of Hoth by stating that she'd "just as soon kiss a Wampa ice creature" than give him a "goodbye kiss."

JEDI MASTER BONUS #4

During the events cinematically chronicled in *Star Wars: A New Hope* and *The Empire Strikes Back,* what were the eight names (mostly derogatory) Han Solo used to address Princess Leia?

---

17. Identify the humiliation Leia was forced to endure by Jabba the Hutt after failing in her efforts to rescue Han from the crime lord's stronghold on Tatooine.

18. What was Leia's response after Luke explained to her the true nature of their relationship and the reality of her heritage?
    A. "Somehow none of this surprises me . . . It's as if I have always known the truth"
    B. "I know. Somehow . . . I've always known"
    C. "I could sense it, Luke . . . don't ask me how I knew, but I just knew"

19. Where were Leia and Luke when he told her the truth that would change her life forever?

JEDI MASTER BONUS #5

What was the number of the detention *block* in which Leia was jailed on the original Death Star battle station?

SMUGGLER'S BLUES: HAN SOLO
Imperial Security Bureau (ISB)
Dossier #1-57566-063-6

1. Identify the star system in which Han was born.

2. To avoid an Imperial blockade, Han dumped a cargo belonging to crime lord Jabba the Hutt. What was in the payload that Solo jettisoned?
    A. Kessel spice
    B. Rubicon ale
    C. Cobakian milk

3. Han won the stocklight freighter, the *Millennium Falcon,* from Lando Calrissian during what kind of high-stakes game of chance?
    A. Jaqquel poker
    B. Nuotok
    C. Sabacc

JEDI MASTER BONUS #1

Han needed to raise enough credits to pay off his debt to Jabba the Hutt. For how many monetary credits did Solo agree to covertly transport Kenobi, Luke, and the two droids to Alderaan, while dodging "Imperial entanglements"?

---

4. After killing Greedo, one of Jabba the Hutt's bounty hunters, what did Han say to the Mos Eisley cantina bartender when he paid him?

5. Which planet was the site of one of Solo's more memorable exploits of piracy, when he and his longtime Wookiee companion, Chewbacca, broke into several immense, well-protected vaults and stole a cache of precious cargo?
   A. Covell
   B. Byss
   C. Gargon

6. (Fill in the Blanks) A skeptical Han told Luke, "Kid, I've flown from one side of this galaxy to the other. I've seen a lot of strange stuff, but I've never seen anything to make me believe there's one all-powerful _____ controlling everything. There's no _____ energy field that controls my destiny."

7. How did Han endanger his friends' lives in the original Death Star's trash compactor?

8. Who accused Han of only taking care of himself and turning his back on the other Rebel pilots during a time when they desperately needed his flying experience?

9. As it turned out, Han could not forsake his newfound friends in their seemingly hopeless battle against the Empire. What reason did he give for showing up just in the nick of time to drive away the TIE starfighters pursuing Luke as he attempted to destroy the Death Star?

10. When Han's debt to Jabba the Hutt went unpaid for three years after the Battle of Yavin, what did the gangster put on Solo's head?

11. What did Han use to slice open the dead Tauntaun on the frozen tundra of the Hoth planet?

JEDI MASTER BONUS #2

Why did Han go out in the extreme, inhospitable cold of Hoth to rescue Luke on a Tauntaun instead of a snowspeeder?

---

12. Although he had a legendary reputation as a smuggler and rogue, who actually called Han a "pirate"?

13. Who was the notorious bounty hunter who tracked Han to Bespin's Cloud City and led Darth Vader to him?

14. What strong metal alloy was Han encased in as a test by Vader?

JEDI MASTER BONUS #3

Identify the medical condition that Han suffered from (temporary blindness, disorientation and weakness) after he was rescued by Princess Leia at Jabba the Hutt's Tatooine desert palace.

---

15. Han agreed to lead the Rebel strike force to the forest moon of Endor in an effort to disable the Imperial shield generator that protected the second Death Star. Who was the first to volunteer to become a member of his command crew aboard the stolen Imperial shuttle *Tydirium*, which Han and his team used to covertly reach Endor's moon?

JEDI MASTER BONUS #4

Who promoted Han to the rank of general in the Alliance to Restore the Republic?

WANTED: DEAD OR ALIVE

If having a price put on his head by crime lord Jabba the Hutt wasn't enough, Han Solo became the prized catch of every bounty hunter in the galaxy when Darth Vader offered an even richer reward to whoever could catch the Corellian-born smuggler and hero of the Rebel Alliance. How familiar are you with this rogues' gallery of bounty hunters, mercenaries, assassin droids, and blasters-for-hire whom Vader turned loose upon the galaxy to track down Solo, his Wookiee partner, and the Millennium Falcon?

1. Where was Boba Fett's starfighter docked at Bespin's Cloud City?
    A. Landing platform 487
    B. The East platform
    C. Outside of the food court plaza

2. Who was the reptilian hired killer contracted by Darth Vader to locate Han Solo after the Battle of Hoth?
    A. Zuckuss
    B. Dengar
    C. Bossk

3. This Rodian bounty hunter finally caught up with Solo in the cantina at Mos Eisley but didn't live to tell about it. Who was he?

4. Identify the galaxy's most infamous mercenary assassin droid who was among the bounty hunters selected by Vader to capture the *Millennium Falcon* and its crew?
   A. AS-20
   B. IG-88
   C. KOS-2

5. (Fill in the Blank) Boba Fett's personally customized starfighter used homing beacons and _____ trackers to keep track of potential prey.

6. Who was the alien bounty hunter commissioned by Darth Vader whose physiology required him to wear a special breathing apparatus when he was away from his homeworld?
   A. Zuckuss
   B. Boushh
   C. Dellalt

JEDI MASTER BONUS #1

As part of an intricate plot to rescue Han Solo from Jabba the Hutt's palace on Tatooine, Princess Leia disguised herself as an Ubese bounty hunter named Boushh. What type of sounds typified the Ubese language?

---

7. Before becoming a ruthless bounty hunter, this rogue droid with a humanoid body and insectoid head was actually a late-model protocol droid. What was its name designation?

8. Identify the scarred Corellian bounty hunter who always wore diverse fragments of battle armor and carried a variety of weapons.
   A. Joruus
   B. Honoghr
   C. Dengar

9. (True or False) 4-LOM and Zuckuss worked as a formidable bounty hunting team.

10. (Fill in the Blank) Boba Fett wore a weapon-covered, armored spacesuit similar to the ones used by the _____ warriors, defeated by the Jedi Knights during the Clone Wars.

11. Which of the following was NOT part of Boba Fett's body armament?
    A. Built-in wrist lasers
    B. Miniature flame throwers
    C. Sonic stunner

12. (True or False) Breedo, a relative of deceased bounty hunter, Greedo, took his next-of-kin's place in Jabba the Hutt's criminal organization on Tatooine.

JEDI MASTER BONUS #2

How many meters in height was the assassin Phlutroid, IG-88?

---

13. (Fill in the Blank) Boba Fett's armored battle suit contained a _____ viewplate and infrared scope.

14. What could be seen dangling from Boba Fett's belt as evidence of his galaxywide reputation as one of the deadliest bounty hunters in the business?

15. Identify the Trandoshan bounty hunter whose basic equipment was a blaster rifle, grenade launcher, and flame thrower?
    A. Bossk
    B. Zuckuss
    C. Gribbet

16. How tall was the 4-LOM droid bounty hunter?

    A. 1.2 meters
    B. 1.6 meters
    C. 2.0 meters

17. (True or False) Zuckuss' standard bounty hunter equipment included protective armor, blaster pistol, vibroblade, and three stun grenades.

18. (Fill in the Blank) Mounted on the chest of Dengar's battle armor was a _____ personal communications transceiver.

19. (Fill in the Blank) Boba Fett's body suit armaments included a _____-projected grappling hook.

20. (True or False) Fett worked both ends of the bounty on Han Solo and accepted exorbitant commissions from both Jabba the Hutt and Darth Vader.

JEDI MASTER BONUS #3

(Fill in the blanks with the correct numbers)

Boba Fett's jet pack could transport the bounty hunter _____ meters horizontally and _____ meters vertically.

JEDI MASTER BONUS #4

Identify the planet on which Han Solo met up with and managed to escape a bounty hunter team dispatched by Jabba the Hutt.

SOLO'S SIDEKICK: CHEWBACCA
Imperial Security Bureau (ISB)
Dossier #0-7860-0315-4

1. Which planet was the homeworld for the Wookiee species?
   A. Gaiinash
   B. Kashyyyk
   C. Etti IV

2. Identify Chewie's two weapons of choice.

3. Besides being an able pilot, what other much-in-demand talent did Chewie possess?

4. (Fill in the blank with the correct number) Wookiees had much longer life expectancies than humans. Chewie was over _____ hundred years old.

5. (True or False) In addition to being chased by bounty hunters working for galactic gangsters like Jabba the Hutt, and wanted by the Empire because of his involvement with Han Solo in the Rebel Alliance, Chewie had also been marked as a fugitive runaway slave.

JEDI MASTER BONUS #1

How many meters in height was Chewie?

---

6. Who was Chewie charged with protecting after Han Solo was captured and encased by Darth Vader in carbonite?

7. Besides being a top-notch mechanic who constantly repaired and upgraded the *Millennium Falcon,* what else did Chewie prove to be adept at mending and renovating?

JEDI MASTER BONUS #2

As he was being lowered into the carbon-freeze chamber by Imperials on Bespin's Cloud City, what did Han say to calm an enraged and roaring Chewie?

---

8. Chewie acted as Han's conscience and often convinced his friend to take an honorable course of action, especially during the Battle of Yavin. What did the Wookiee do to help ensure this first major tactical victory for the Rebel Alliance?

9. What major role did Chewie play during the Galactic Civil War's most decisive engagement on the forest moon of Endor?

10. Like all Wookiees, Chewie had limited vocal ability, which made it impossible for him to speak anything other than his own language. Chewie's dialect was comprised of a series of what type of sounds?

11. Chewie was an important asset during the rescue of Princess Leia aboard the original Death Star. What key part did he play that allowed Han and Luke the opportunity to infiltrate the battle station's detention block?

12. Who accompanied Chewie on the *Millennium Falcon*'s return trip to Tatooine to await Luke Skywalker and the rest of his friends as they planned their rescue of Han Solo from Jabba the Hutt's desert palace?

JEDI MASTER BONUS #3

What action did Chewie take on Endor's forest moon that caused the Wookiee, Han, Luke and the droids to become ensnared in a suspended Ewok net?

BEHIND-THE-SCENES
The Empire Strikes Back

1. Where was the scene filmed in which a swamp creature on the planet Dagobah grabbed R2-D2?
    A. A bog outside of Shreveport, Louisiana
    B. The Florida Everglades
    C. George Lucas' unfinished swimming pool

2. (True or False) Over 150 models were used in the filming of the *Star Wars* trilogy's second installment.

3. Who was the actor from the long-running NBC comedy, *Cheers*, who briefly appeared in the movie as Rebel Major Derlin during the Hoth base evacuation scene?
    A. Woody Harrelson
    B. John Ratzenberger
    C. Kelsey Grammer

4. What vegetable did the ILM special effects crew place in the film as a little "inside joke" during the asteroid belt scene with the *Millennium Falcon?*

5. (True or False) Lucas was concerned with preventing leaks about the movie, especially the catwalk scene in which Darth Vader told Luke Skywalker that he was his father. The line David Prowse actually spoke during filming was "Obi-Wan

Kenobi is your father," rather than "I am your father," which was dubbed into the movie's final print during postproduction.

6. Who played the Rebel soldiers manning the ground emplacements during the Hoth base assault scenes?
    A. The Norwegian Red Cross Rescue Skiers
    B. Members of the Norwegian Olympic bobsled team
    C. Extras from a Soviet movie filming in Norway

JEDI MASTER BONUS #1

What two types of snakes were used in the filming of the Dagobah swamp planet scenes?

---

7. Which natural disaster caused the camera crew to be delayed in Norway (where the Hoth scenes were filmed)?
    A. Blizzard
    B. Avalanche
    C. Ice storm

8. Who were the screenwriters for this second installment of the *Star Wars* saga?

9. (True or False) The scene with the Imperial probot conducting reconnaissance on the Hoth planet was filmed with a miniature *and* a full-size model.

10. When did principal photography begin on *The Empire Strikes Back?*
    A. November 21, 1978
    B. March 5, 1979
    C. May 30, 1979

11. Where was the movie's soundtrack recorded?

  A. Stonehenge Audio-Visual, Inc., in Surrey, England
  B. Wolf 359 Studios in Lasdale, England
  C. Anvil Recording Studios in Denham, England

12. (True or False) The special effects crew studied elephants to ensure that the movements of the Imperial AT-ATs seemed as realistic as possible.

JEDI MASTER BONUS #2

The designers at ILM wanted to utilize a radical design for Boba Fett's ship, *Slave I*. What did the F/X crew end up using as the bounty hunter's starfighter and where did they get it?

---

13. What scene was later written into the script as a result of the accident in which Mark Hamill went through the windshield of his BMW?

14. Who was the director of *The Empire Strikes Back?*

15. (True or False) The release date for the film was May 27, 1980.

16. Besides his reputation, what else did George Lucas stake on the success of his sequel to *Star Wars: A New Hope?*

17. As executive producer of the movie, where did Lucas remain while filming was underway in England?

18. (True or False) Irvin Kershner originally declined Lucas' offer to direct *The Empire Strikes Back.*

19. How many sets were built for the movie?
  A. 52
  B. 64
  C. 71

20. (True or False) With the exception of the first ten days in Norway, the film was shot inside movie studios.

JEDI MASTER BONUS #3

In a scene filmed but later cut, Han Solo, Princess Leia and C-3PO were shown running through a corridor of the Rebel base on Hoth. Han attempted to take a shortcut through a door with a sign on it, but Leia warned him, "That's where those [Wampa ice] creatures are kept." Before running off into another direction, which character ripped off the sign, hoping that invading Imperial stormtroopers would enter the room?

---

21. Which actor was constantly reminding Director Kershner that the special effects' epic proportions were overshadowing the performances by the cast?
    A. Alec Guinness
    B. Billy Dee Williams
    C. Harrison Ford

22. (Fill in the blank with the correct number) The floor of the Dagobah set was about _____ feet above the actual floor of the stage.

23. Identify the second-unit director of *The Empire Strikes Back* who helmed the ice-planet Hoth sequences on location in Norway.
    A. Peter MacDonald
    B. John Everett
    C. Samuel Holcomb

24. How long did Director Kershner spend in England storyboarding the script before actual filming began?
    A. Six months
    B. Eight months
    C. One year

25. (True or False) Frank Oz and his crew manipulated the Yoda puppet individually: one person operated the creature's ears, another blinked his eyes, another person would move the mouth, still another would move an arm and so on.

26. Which national publication's cover on May 19, 1980, pictured an artist's rendition of Darth Vader with the screaming headline "The Empire Strikes Back!"?
    A. *People*
    B. *Time*
    C. *Newsweek*

27. Identify the writer who adapted *The Empire Strikes Back* for National Public Radio.

28. Who described Darth Vader in interviews for the *Star Wars* sequel as "much more developed, but just as nasty as ever"?

29. (True or False) A scene was cut from the final print of the movie in which R2-D2 encountered a Wampa ice creature within the Rebel base on Hoth.

30. Who changed Han Solo's scripted reply to Leia's "I love you" from "I love you, too" to "I know" during the scene in which the Corellian smuggler was about to be frozen in carbonite by Darth Vader?
    A. George Lucas
    B. Harrison Ford
    C. Carrie Fisher

JEDI MASTER BONUS #4

Identify the magazine whose July 7, 1980, cover was graced with a photo of the four major stars in costume from *The Empire Strikes Back* with the headline: "Empire's Fab Four."

JEDI MASTER BONUS #5

How many TV monitors were utilized by Frank Oz and his crew in order to give them instant feedback on their performances with the various parts of the Yoda puppet?

---

31. (True or False) Lighting for the special effects was so intense that several models melted.

32. (Fill in the blank with the correct city) The design for the Imperial AT-ATs was based on a ship-loading structure in a(n) _____, California, shipyard.

33. (True or False) George Lucas was so concerned with security surrounding the plot of *The Empire Strikes Back* that he kept the major actors in the dark and, according to Carrie Fisher, even distributed script pages for secret scenes on special color-coded pages in sealed envelopes, and asked the crew *not to listen* on the day the scenes were shot.

34. Who said in interviews promoting the movie that Lando Calrissian "transcends questions, stereotypes, cliches. He's a pop figure and a pop figure can go anywhere he wants to go"?

35. Who stated publicly, "Somebody suggested ["the Other" with the Force] might be the princess. I think that would be a letdown"?
    A. Carrie Fisher
    B. Mark Hamill
    C. Alec Guinness

36. Which four characters made a joint guest appearance on *The Muppet Show* as part of the promotional campaign for *The Empire Strikes Back?*

      A. Luke, Leia, Han and Lando
      B. Luke, Chewie, R2-D2 and C-3PO
      C. Han, Chewie, Yoda and Darth Vader

37. Who was the producer for *The Empire Strikes Back?*

38. Identify the author of *The Empire Strikes Back* novelization.
      A. Donald F. Glut
      B. Timothy Zahn
      C. James Kahn

JEDI MASTER BONUS #6

What two Academy Awards did the movie win?

JEDI MASTER BONUS #7

How long did it take John Williams and the London Symphony Orchestra to record the score for the film?

JEDI MASTER BONUS #8

How many minutes of music did Williams compose for *The Empire Strikes Back?*

---

39. (Fill in the blank with the correct number) George Lucas financed the *Star Wars* sequel himself, borrowing heavily to cover the _____ million dollar production cost.

40. (True or False) An advance version of the movie had a sequence in which a snowspeeder crashed directly into the head of an Imperial "walker."

41. What did George Lucas consider the "biggest problem" in writing the storyline for *The Empire Strikes Back?*

42. Why did Lucas refer to the movie as a "darker film" than its predecessor?
    - A. The saga's heroes were placed into the "worst positions of their lives . . . a black hole."
    - B. "The good guys lost and the bad guys won."
    - C. "Luke learned that Obi-Wan lied to him" and that "Darth Vader was his father."

43. Name the puppet master Lucas initially offered the opportunity to imbue the wise, elfin Jedi master, Yoda, with life and character.

44. Who did Lucas consider "the most wonderful collaborator" during the filming of *The Empire Strikes Back?*
    - A. Director Irvin Kershner
    - B. Producer Gary Kurtz
    - C. Composer John Williams

45. (True or False) Lucas originally wanted to use existing classical music for the movie's soundtrack.

46. (True or False) Lucas intended the climactic catwalk scene between Darth Vader and Luke Skywalker to be ambiguous, leaving the audience wondering whether Vader had told Luke the truth about his heritage.

JEDI MASTER BONUS #9

Although *The Empire Strikes Back: The Special Edition* featured an enhanced and completely restored print as well as a new digitally recorded THX soundtrack, only a few special effects shots were upgraded from the original version. Even though Lucas believed that the original film version "stood up pretty well, all the matte paintings and everything else," which scenes were "punched up" in *The Special Edition* with the in-camera recompositing of a few shots and Ralph McQuarrie's series of mattes?

---

47. The full-scale Imperial probot replica was inspired by an image created by which renowned visionary graphic artist?
    A. Jacque Nouveau
    B. Jean "Moebius" Giraud
    C. Frances LeBlanc

48. Identify the production facility outside of London where the movie's soundstage work was filmed.

49. How long was the Wampa ice creature puppet on screen?
    A. Less than a second
    B. Two seconds
    C. Three seconds

50. The Imperial "walkers" were animated on a special miniature ILM set complete with a painted, cloudy blue sky backing. What did the visual effects technicians use as snow to dress the battlefield?
    A. Flour
    B. Baking soda
    C. A shaving cream/white sand mixture

51. (True or False) *The Empire Strikes Back* required 600 to 700 optical composites, as compared to 380 effects shots for the first installment of the *Star Wars* trilogy.

52. (True or False) Frank Oz and his crew animated the Yoda creature by working the puppet from underneath the stage through hidden openings in the set.

JEDI MASTER BONUS #10

(Fill in the Blank)

George Lucas described Bespin's Cloud City as "a kind of Flash Gordon city floating in the sky on a _____."

---

53. How many feet long was the *Executor* special effects model?
    A. Six
    B. Eight
    C. Ten

54. Who created the Wampa ice creature hand puppet?
    A. Jack Bergstrom
    B. Jon Berg
    C. Dick Dahlquist

55. Identify the special effects model that was the first ship in the movie trilogy to be made out of strong, but lightweight, honeycombed aluminum.

56. (Fill in the Blank) George Lucas has acknowledged that the mythic principles of the Force, as taught to Luke Skywalker by Jedi master Yoda in *The Empire Strikes Back*, were actually inspired by the Chinese concept of _____, which is believed to be a universal energy force.

JEDI MASTER BONUS #11

Who operated the *Millennium Falcon*-swallowing space slug creature, which was in reality nothing more than a glorified hand puppet?

JEDI MASTER BONUS #12

Who built the compositing system utilized so heavily in the movie?

JEDI MASTER BONUS #13

The green-skinned Yoda creature came to life only after a long series of design-stage evolutions. What color was the Jedi master's skin in the early concept sketches?

JEDI MASTER BONUS #14

Although the early designs of Yoda ranged from snow-bearded Santa Claus-ish figures to lively elves, who sculpted the final Yoda puppet that appeared in *The Empire Strikes Back?*

JEDI MASTER BONUS #15

Initially, the Imperial AT-ATs were to take the form of Norwegian army tanks shot on location. Identify the two stop motion animators who created the AT-ATs as puppet models from Joe Johnston's designs of four-legged mechanical monsters.

JEDI MASTER BONUS #16

What region of Norway served as the major location shoot for the ice planet Hoth scenes?

THE NAME GAME
The Empire Strikes Back

Match the name of the actor with the corresponding character they portrayed in the second installment of the Star Wars *trilogy.*

---

1. _____	Kenneth Colley	A.	Captain Needa
2. _____	Bruce Boa	B.	Zev
3. _____	Jeremy Bulloch	C.	Rebel Deck Lieutenant
4. _____	John Hollis	D.	Lobot
5. _____	Julian Colley	E.	Admiral Piett
6. _____	Michael Culver	F.	Wedge
7. _____	Michael Sheard	G.	Dak
8. _____	Jake McKenzie	H.	General Rieekan
9. _____	Ian Liston	I.	Admiral Ozzel
10. _____	Dennis Lawson	J.	General Veers
11. _____	John Morton	K.	Boba Fett
12. _____	Christopher Malcom	L.	Janson

JEDI MASTER BONUS #1

Who provided the voice for the Emperor?

JEDI MASTER BONUS #2

Identify the supporting cast member who played the Chief Ugnaught.

JEDI MASTER BONUS #3

Who was listed in the film's credits as the performing assistant for Yoda?

JEDI MASTER BONUS #4

Which one of the following did NOT perform in a supporting role as an Imperial officer: John Dicks, Robin Scobey, Mark Jones, Milton Johns, Coburn Howard or Oliver Maguire?

REBELS WITH A CAUSE

The Rebel Alliance to Restore the Republic consisted of entire star systems, solitary worlds, and even dissident groups and individuals from otherwise impartial or Empire-allied planets, all united in their opposition to the tyranny and oppression of the Galactic Empire and its New Order. The goal of the Alliance was well known throughout the universe, but how well do you know its Rebel members?

1. Identify Luke Skywalker's childhood friend from Tatooine who piloted an X-wing in the Rebel attempt to destroy the original Death Star battle station.

2. What was the comm-unit designation for Luke Skywalker's X-wing starfighter during the Battle of Yavin?
   A. Red Four
   B. Red Five
   C. Red Six

3. Which Alliance commander was put in charge of the X-wing starfighter group after Red Leader's death during the Battle of Yavin?
   A. Narra
   B. Willard
   C. Fyre

4. Identify the Rebel gunner who died when Luke Skywalker's snowspeeder took a hit from AT-AT weapon fire during the assault by Imperial forces on Hoth.

5. Who was the lead pilot of the Rebel Y-wing Gold Squadron during the Battle of Yavin?

6. Who was the general who planned and coordinated the full-scale assault on the original Death Star?
   A. Rieekan
   B. Madine
   C. Dodonna

JEDI MASTER BONUS #1

Identify the isolated Rebel sentry outpost on Hoth that was destroyed by an Imperial probot.

---

7. Name the former senior Senator of the Old Republic who later was elected as the leader of the Alliance to Restore the Republic.

8. (Fill in the Blank) All Rebel warriors were ordered to withdraw from combat and return to base when an Alliance Battle Staff officer issued the code _____ Signal.
   A. Delphi
   B. Omega
   C. Quasar

9. Identify the advance lookout station for the Rebel base on Hoth whose soldiers were first to detect the invading Imperial forces.
   A. Station Theta
   B. Sentry Beto
   C. Outpost Beta

10. (True or False) Red Leader was the Rebel pilot who made the first attempt to hit the original Death Star during the Battle of Yavin.

11. What evidence did Darth Vader have that Princess Leia and the Blockade Runner were not on a diplomatic mission as she claimed?

12. This admiral's principal military specialization was in the field of Imperial defense procedures, and he served as one of Mon Mothma's two senior Rebel advisers. Who was he?

JEDI MASTER BONUS #2

What was the name of the veteran Rebel Y-wing pilot whose comm-unit designation during the battle to destroy the original Death Star was Gold Five?

---

13. What was Porkin's X-wing comm-unit designation during the Battle of Yavin?
    A. Red Four
    B. Blue Five
    C. Red Six

14. (True or False) Red Four was the comm-unit designation for Rebel pilot Wedge Antilles' X-wing during the Battle of Yavin.

15. Which Alliance commander died when the Rebel convoy he and his starfighter squadron were escorting was ambushed by Imperial forces near Derra IV?
    A. Narra
    B. Antilles
    C. Willard

16. (True or False) Tarrin was a Rebel pilot who served in Luke Skywalker's X-wing squadron during the Battle of Hoth.

17. Who was the Rebel pilot who found and rescued Luke Sky-
    walker and Han Solo after they were forced to spend the night
    on the surface of the ice planet Hoth?
    A. Dak
    B. Janson
    C. Zev

JEDI MASTER BONUS #3

What was the evacuation code signal for the Rebel troops on
Hoth?

JEDI MASTER BONUS #4

What was the code name for the clandestine Alliance mission
that sent Princess Leia and the Blockade Runner to retrieve
the technical readouts of the original Death Star?

---

18. During which conflict of the Galactic Civil War did Rebel pilot
    Porkin die?
    A. Battle of Yavin
    B. Battle of Hoth
    C. Battle of Endor

19. Although most of the younger Rebel pilots called him by his
    comm-unit designation, what was Red Leader's real name?
    A. Bryan
    B. Michael
    C. Dave

20. During which battle were Red Leader and his wingmen killed?

21. What was Rebel pilot John D's X-wing comm-unit designation
    during the Battle of Yavin?

22. What was Biggs Darklighter's X-wing comm-unit designation during the battle to destroy the first Death Star battle station?
    A. Blue Two
    B. Red Three
    C. Green Four

23. (Fill in the Blank) Commander Narra was affectionately known as "The _____" by the X-wing fighter squadron to which Luke Skywalker belonged.

24. After the Battle of Yavin, who commanded the legendary X-wing group of starfighter pilots known as the Rogue Squadron?

25. Identify the Rebel general and covert operations specialist who plotted and carried out the capture of the Imperial shuttle, *Tydirium*, and trained Han Solo's Rebel strike team to clandestinely reach the forest moon of Endor.

JEDI MASTER BONUS #5

Identify the Rebel officer who was referred to as Echo 7 during *The Empire Strikes Back.*

---

26. Who was the high-ranking Alliance officer responsible for all Rebel ground and fleet forces in the Hoth system?
    A. Major Derlin
    B. General Rieekan
    C. General Madine

27. (True or False) Gold Leader was the commander of the Gold Wing starfighter battle squadron during the Battle of Hoth.

28. (Fill in the blank with the correct number) Gray Wing was one of _____ principal Rebel starfighter squadrons participating in *The Return of the Jedi*'s Battle of Endor.

29. What was Rebel pilot Wedge Antilles' snowspeeder comm-unit designation in *Return of the Jedi?*
    A. Rogue Three
    B. Green Two
    C. Rogue Leader

30. Who was the only Rebel pilot besides Luke Skywalker to appear in both *Star Wars* and *The Empire Strikes Back?*

31. How many X-wing starfighters constituted the Rebel Alliance's legendary Rogue Squadron?
    A. Ten
    B. Twelve
    C. Fifteen

JEDI MASTER BONUS #6

Who presented Princess Leia with the Heroes of Yavin medallions at the conclusion of *Star Wars?*

---

32. (True or False) During the Battle of Endor, the comm-unit designation for Blue Leader's second-in-command was Blue Wing.

33. (Fill in the Blank) Blue Squad was one of many _____ starfighter groups in the Rebel's Blue Wing attack force during the Battle of Endor.

34. Identify the comm-unit designation for the Rebel Alliance's hidden command headquarters on Hoth.

35. In which year was Mon Mothma, Senator and Rebel leader, born?
    A. 55 BSW4
    B. 50 BSW4
    C. 48 BSW4

36. (True or False) Green Leader was the comm-unit designation for the commander of one of the four primary Rebel starfighter battle squadrons during the decisive Battle of Endor.

37. (True or False) Green Leader's second-in-command died during a Rebel assault on an Imperial communications ship.

38. Name the veteran Rebel pilot whose comm-unit designation was Rogue Four during the Battle of Hoth.

JEDI MASTER BONUS #7

During the Battle of Hoth, who was the gunner on the snowspeeder piloted by Wedge Antilles?

---

39. What equipment did the Rebels use to bring down the AT-AT walker?

40. (Fill in the Blank) The Empire commonly referred to the Rebel Alliance as the _____.

41. What was General Madine's first name?

42. What was Rebel pilot Tiree's Y-wing comm-unit designation during the assault against the original Death Star?
    A. Gold Two
    B. Blue Three
    C. Red One

43. What was the code name cover of the Rebel pilots assigned to protect an Alliance convoy of badly needed supplies to the Hoth base?
    A. Relentless One
    B. Freedom Train
    C. Renegade Flight

44. What was the code name cover for the Rebel starfighter pilots responsible for protecting the evacuating troops during the invasion of Imperial forces at the Hoth base?
    A. Distance Run
    B. Ice Flight
    C. Rogue Flight

45. What were the colors of the Rebel pilot's flight suits in *Star Wars* and *The Empire Strikes Back?*

JEDI MASTER BONUS #8

When Luke Skywalker elected to resign his commission, who was the expert X-wing pilot who took command of the elite Rogue Squadron and led the assault against the second Death Star battle station?

ALIEN FACES & PLACES
Part II

1. (True or False) Beranda was the name of one of Jabba the Hutt's guards, killed when Luke Skywalker and his friends rescued Han Solo from the gangster's desert stronghold on Tatooine.

2. Name the alien beast indigenous to Endor's moon that had a rotund, furry body with elongated legs and a mouthful of razor-sharp, extruding teeth.
   A. Retelian
   B. Wiipoly
   C. Yuzzum

3. Which tropical moon of Yavin once housed a covert Rebel base in the ruins of a Massassi temple?

4. Identify the leather-skinned humanoid species who traditionally wore a solitary plaited topknot on one side of their bald heads.
   A. Thaladon
   B. Weequay
   C. Queevox

5. Name the Alderaanian continent on which the rural Uplands were located.

A. Klaz
B. Uuipor
C. Thon

6. Which alien world did the Rebel Alliance utilize as a remote location to conceal the stolen technical schematics for the Empire's first Death Star battle station?

JEDI MASTER BONUS #1

(Fill in the blank dialogue)

Han Solo attempted to boost Luke Skywalker's spirits after his recovery from the Wampa ice creature attack by telling the boy, "You look strong enough to pull the ears off a _____."

---

7. (True or False) Tin-Tin Dwarfs were a bipedal race of rodent-like beings who stood less than a meter high.

8. Name the rugged, S-shaped valley on Tatooine where Luke Skywalker flew his T-16 skyhopper.

9. In which star system was the Cloud City mining colony located?

10. Identify the carnivorous, winged creatures with rock-crushing teeth that inhabited the scorching desert sands of Tatooine.
    A. Bonegnawers
    B. Bonecrushers
    C. Bonebiters

11. (True or False) The swampy and junglelike planet of Dagobah was located in the sparsely populated Zaytar star system.

12. Name the alien with twin skull appendages ("head tails") who served as Jabba the Hutt's majordomo.

JEDI MASTER BONUS #2

Identify the planet whose proximity to its sun created solar mirages of encircling fire rings.

---

13. These somewhat slow, but fierce and determined, sentries in Jabba the Hutt's lair on Tatooine were green-skinned, and had piglike snouts and tusks. Which species of aliens were these palace guards?
    A. H'doreans
    B. Gamorreans
    C. Yacodians

14. (True or False) Gravel storms frequently subjected Tatooine to violent wind tempests which whipped rocks and sand through the air at dangerously high speeds.

15. This immense alien biped wore a frayed robe and was employed by galactic gangster Jabba the Hutt. What was his name?
    A. Hermi Odle
    B. Quill-Face Neeva
    C. Jiija

16. (True or False) Only one life-form was known to exist on the frozen world of Hoth.

17. (True or False) Ishi Tib was a quadruped alien with an elongated, disproportionate snout who served as a member of Jabba the Hutt's court.

18. Identify the Dune Sea-bordering canyon in which the vagabond tribal Sand People resided on Tatooine.
    A. Grawyler Pass
    B. Jundland Wastes
    C. Echols Valley

JEDI MASTER BONUS #3

What warning did the Mos Eisley cantina bartender issue when Luke Skywalker and Ben Kenobi confronted the alien clientele?

---

19. (Fill in the Blank) Domesticated _____ were herbivores cared for by herders and raised primarily as a meat source, although their hides had many uses throughout the galaxy.

20. Identify the repulsive, goat-faced alien with three eyes who was a member of Jabba the Hutt's criminal entourage.
    A. Veehod
    B. Tessek
    C. Ree-Yees

21. Name the Kowakian lizard-monkey who served as Jabba the Hutt's court jester and sat at the base of the bloated criminal kingpin's throne.

22. (Fill in the Blank) Turbulent atmospheric conditions known as _____ occasionally devastated the deserts of Tatooine.

23. What was the informal name for the alien race easily identified by the four tentacles protruding from their jaws?
    A. Octopus Terrain Dwellers
    B. Squid Heads
    C. Four Arms

24. Identify the star system where the Rebels' convoy of military spacecraft rendezvoused prior to the decisive Battle of Endor.
    A. Rydrox
    B. Dreelian
    C. Sullust

JEDI MASTER BONUS #4

What was the memorable physical characteristic of the alien who followed Luke Skywalker and the others into the Mos Eisley cantina and then reported them to Imperial stormtroopers?

---

25. Identify the domesticated creatures used as riding and pack animals by the Rebel Alliance during their tenure on the Hoth planet.

26. Luke Skywalker grew up on a moisture farm outside of this quiet and peaceful community on Tatooine. Name the town.

27. (Fill in the Blank) Tatooine's expansive desert wasteland, the _____ Sea, was at one time an immense body of water.

28. Identify the royal house that presided over Alderaan's legislative High Council.
    A. The High Court
    B. The Supreme Majesty
    C. The Prime Council

29. (True or False) Jabba the Hutt was approximately four meters in length, which was mammoth even among his own species.

30. (True or False) The reptilian Rancor beast in Jabba's palace pit was six meters in height when it stood upright on its two legs.

JEDI MASTER BONUS #5

What color was the jumpsuit of an Ugnaught laborer on Bespin's Cloud City?

---

31. How many rows of razor-sharp teeth lined the large mouth of the omnivorous and multitentacled Sarlacc creature?
    A. Two
    B. Three
    C. Four

32. In which star system was the desert world of Tatooine located?

33. Identify the rare gas derived from Bespin's atmosphere and refined at Cloud City.
    A. Mithoc
    B. Niloktian
    C. Tibanna

34. How many Sand People raided Luke Skywalker's landspeeder on Tatooine?

35. How many spikes were atop a Tusken Raider's head?

36. What was the fate of the band of Jawas that sold R2-D2 and C-3PO to Luke Skywalker and his uncle?

JEDI MASTER BONUS #6

How many years were required for the Sarlacc creature's digestive juices to break down food?

---

37. What color was a Tauntaun?

38. Which gender of Banthas had long, paired, spiral-shaped horns protruding from their heads?

39. Bestine was not only a planetary ally of the Rebel Alliance, it was also the name of a small farming community on which planet?

   A. Beru
   B. Tatooine
   C. Cyhoj

40. (True or False) Bocce was one of many languages spoken on Tatooine.

41. (True or False) The huge dewback reptilian creatures were herbivores.

42. How many horns protruded from the foreheads of the humanoid Nikto species?
   A. Two
   B. Three
   C. Four

JEDI MASTER BONUS #7

Identify the silicon-based creatures who attacked the *Millennium Falcon* when it was inside the space slug.

---

43. Did the alien called Snaggletooth appear in the Mos Eisley cantina scene in *Star Wars* or Jabba the Hutt's court in *Return of the Jedi?*

44. (True or False) The garage/workshop residential extensions on Tatooine and other settlement worlds were called biotech domes.

45. (True or False) The t'ill was a blossoming plant indigenous to Endor's forest moon.

46. (Fill in the blank with the correct number) The Sarlacc creature's enormous mucous-coated mouth measured more than _____ meters in diameter.

A. 1.9
B. 2.5
C. 3.1

JEDI MASTER BONUS #8

What star system was the *Millennium Falcon* in when the freighter and its crew floated away with the Star Destroyer's garbage?

---

47. On which planet did Luke Skywalker's boyhood friend, Biggs Darklighter, first make contact with the Rebellion?
    A. Bestine
    B. Givin
    C. Batcheela

48. Who did the Mos Eisley bartender say the criminal-infested cantina would not serve?

49. Identify the repulsive, toadlike creature with a lightning-fast tongue that lived outside Jabba's palace on Tatooine.
    A. Terak
    B. Worrt
    C. Joben

JEDI MASTER BONUS #9

What alien race's females were known throughout the galaxy for their exotic dancing?

JEDI MASTER BONUS #10

In what sector of the Outer Rim Territories was the Dagobah system located?

LORD OF THE DARK SIDE: DARTH VADER
Bothan Spy Network (BSN) Dossier #97653-012

1. Anakin Skywalker was a hero of what dreadful conflict that erupted during the time of the Old Republic (approximately thirty-five years prior to the events leading up to the Battle of Yavin)?

2. Who fine-tuned Anakin's inherent ability to use the Force to near perfection before the Jedi Knight was seduced by the dark side and transformed into the "twisted and evil" Darth Vader?

3. (Fill in the blank dialogue) Luke Skywalker's uncle Owen was afraid that the boy would grow up to be just like his father, Anakin, an "_____ dreamer."

4. Who described Anakin as "the greatest star pilot in the galaxy" and "a cunning warrior"?

5. How did the newly transformed Darth Vader, servant and emissary of the Emperor, sustain the injuries that later required him to wear life-supporting armor?

6. As the Emperor's ambassador to the New Order, what brutal task did Darth Vader perform for his new master during the last days of the Old Republic?

JEDI MASTER BONUS #1

Identify the mysterious and fear-inducing cabal of which Vader was a member and "Dark Lord."

---

7. When Vader told Governor Tarkin aboard the original Death Star battle station that "this will be a day long remembered," to what was he referring besides Obi-Wan Kenobi's death?

8. Prior to his death in Luke Skywalker's arms, who was the only other person to have seen Vader without his life-support helmet and breath mask?
   A. General Veers
   B. Admiral Ozzel
   C. Admiral Piett

9. Where did Vader wear his lightsaber when it was not in use?

10. What was his full title?

11. How did Imperial officers address Vader?

12. Identify the military command that Vader was given after the destruction of the original Death Star by Luke Skywalker and the Rebel starfighter assault force.

JEDI MASTER BONUS #2

Where was Vader's private, spherical, meditation chamber located?

---

13. What fate did Vader initially plan for Princess Leia and Chewbacca on Bespin's Cloud City, and how did he alter it?

14. During his first one-on-one battle with Luke Skywalker, what did Vader use in the duel in addition to his lightsaber?

15. What was Vader's secret agenda after he converted Luke to the dark side of the Force?

JEDI MASTER BONUS #3

What was Vader's comm-unit designation for his personal *Lambda*-class shuttle?

JEDI MASTER BONUS #4

In the end, Vader came full circle and died a noble death as Anakin Skywalker because of Luke's faith in "the good" within Vader's black metal shell. With his mask removed and a painful smile creasing his scarred and elderly face, what were Anakin Skywalker's final words to his son?

REBEL RUMBLINGS & IMPERIAL TRANSMISSIONS
The Empire Strikes Back

1. (Fill in the Blank) When Luke Skywalker asked Yoda about his friends' destinies, "Future? Will they die?" Yoda answered, "Difficult to see. Always in _____ is the future."

2. (Fill in the Blank) Darth Vader congratulated Luke Skywalker during their climactic lightsaber duel: "Impressive . . . most impressive. Obi-Wan has taught you well. You have controlled your _____ . . . now release your anger."

3. Who told Han Solo, "A death mark's not an easy thing to live with. You're a good fighter, Solo. I hate to lose you"?

4. Who called Han Solo a "natural leader"?
    A. General Rieekan
    B. Princess Leia
    C. Lando Calrissian

5. (True or False) General Veers informed Darth Vader, "Comscan has detected an energy field protecting an area around the fifth planet of the Hoth system. The field is strong enough to deflect any bombardment."

6. Who referred to Luke Skywalker as "a new enemy"?

JEDI MASTER BONUS #1

What was Yoda's response when Luke asked the Jedi Master if the dark side of the Force was stronger than that of the light?

---

7. Who called the bounty hunters that Darth Vader hired "scum"?

    A. Han Solo
    B. Captain Piett
    C. Admiral Ozzel

8. Who said, "Surrender is a perfectly acceptable alternative in extreme circumstances"?

    A. Yoda
    B. Han Solo
    C. C-3PO

9. Which character described Lando Calrissian as "a card player, gambler, scoundrel"?

    A. Princess Leia
    B. Han Solo
    C. C-3PO

10. (Fill in the Blank) On the landing platform of Cloud City, Lando eyed Han carefully and shook his head. "Why, you slimy, double-crossing, no-good _____! You've got a lot of guts coming here, after what you pulled."

11. Who counseled Luke that it was "a dangerous time" for him, when he would be "tempted by the dark side of the Force"?

12. (Fill in the Blank) Yoda warned Luke before he departed hastily from Dagobah, "Only a fully trained Jedi Knight with the Force as his ally will _____ Vader and his Emperor."

13. Who was worried that Luke would "become an agent of evil" if he chose "the quick and easy path, as Vader did"?

14. (True or False) Lando Calrissian slapped Han on the back and said sarcastically, "You certainly have a way with people."

JEDI MASTER BONUS #2

(Fill in the Blank)

When Lando informed Darth Vader that carbon freezing might kill Luke Skywalker, the Dark Lord replied, "I do not want the Emperor's _____ damaged. We will test it . . . on Captain Solo."

---

15. Who told Luke, "The Force is with you, young Skywalker"?

16. Which character boasted, "I'm full of surprises"?
    A. Han Solo
    B. Luke Skywalker
    C. Lando Calrissian

17. Who called Chewie "a hairy beast"?
    A. Han Solo
    B. Princess Leia
    C. C-3PO

18. (Fill in the Blank) Darth Vader tried to persuade Luke to give in to the power of the dark side of the Force by pleading, "Join me and I will complete your training. With our combined strength, we can end this destructive _____ and bring order to the galaxy."

19. What did Vader consider Luke's "destiny"?

20. Who was warned not "to trust a strange computer"?

JEDI MASTER BONUS #3

What five words were the last that Darth Vader telepathically spoke to Luke Skywalker in the second installment of the *Star Wars* trilogy?

21. Who called the Hoth planet an "ice cube"?

22. Identify the character who referred to Chewie as a "fuzz ball"?
    A. Han Solo
    B. Princess Leia
    C. Lando Calrissian

23. During the Imperial assault on Hoth, who "felt surprise was wiser" and ordered a fleet of Star Destroyers to emerge from hyperspace?

24. Name the overly confident Rebel who bragged to Luke that he felt he "could take on the whole Empire" himself.

25. Who ordered the head controller at Echo Base to "give the evacuation code and get to your transports"?
    A. General Rieekan
    B. Princess Leia
    C. Han Solo

26. (True or False) Lando Calrissian, the former owner of the *Millennium Falcon*, referred to his old ship as a "bucket of bolts."

27. Who called Han's plan of hiding the *Millennium Falcon* in an asteroid field "suicide"?
    A. C-3PO
    B. Princess Leia
    C. Darth Vader

28. (Fill in the Blank) Han slowly pulled Leia close to him in a tight embrace and said in a low, seductive voice, "You like me because I'm a _____."

JEDI MASTER BONUS #4

What two words did Luke use to describe Dagobah, which offended Yoda because the Jedi Master considered the swamp planet his "home"?

---

29. (True or False) The Emperor acknowledged to Darth Vader that the Force was strong with Luke and if he could be turned to the dark side "he would become a powerful ally."

30. Which explanation did Yoda give Obi-Wan for why he couldn't teach Luke to be a Jedi?
    A. "The boy has no patience."
    B. "He has no willingness to learn."
    C. "He will not open himself up to the ways of the Force."

31. Who confessed, "I have a bad feeling about this"?
    A. Luke Skywalker
    B. Princess Leia
    C. Han Solo

32. Identify the character who said angrily, "I am not a committee!"

33. Who called a Mynock a "beastly thing" when one of the bat-like creatures flapped its wings loudly against the cockpit window of the *Millennium Falcon?*
    A. Princess Leia
    B. Han Solo
    C. C-3PO

34. (Fill in the Blank) When Luke asked Yoda how he could tell the good side of the Force from the bad, the Jedi Master

replied, "When you are at calm, at peace. Passive. A Jedi uses the Force for _____ and defense, never for attack."

JEDI MASTER BONUS #5

What four words did Yoda use to describe the huge, dead, black tree that was "strong with the dark side of the Force"?

---

35. (Fill in the Blank) Darth Vader instructed the rogue's gallery of galactic bounty hunters: ". . . there will be a substantial reward for the one who finds the *Millennium Falcon*. You are free to use any _____ necessary, but I want them alive."

36. Identify the Imperial officer who said, "They can't have disappeared. No ship that small has a cloaking device" when told that the *Millennium Falcon* no longer appeared on their tracking scopes.
    A. Admiral Ozzel
    B. Captain Needa
    C. Admiral Piett

37. (True or False) As part of Luke Skywalker's Jedi training, Yoda instructed the boy to "unlearn what you have learned."

38. Which character proved he could not be trusted, even though he had "no love for the Empire"?

39. Who laughingly called Han Solo an "old pirate"?

40. What reason did Obi-Wan Kenobi give Luke for why his friends were "made to suffer"?
    A. "Vader knows you are strong in the Force."
    B. "The Emperor wants to turn you to the dark side."
    C. "It is you and your abilities the Emperor wants."

41. What was Obi-Wan's parting advice to Luke before he left Dagobah for Bespin's Cloud City?

JEDI MASTER BONUS #6

(Fill in the Blank)

After R2-D2's circuits lit up and smoke began to seep out from underneath his squat, cylindrical body, C-3PO shot back defensively, "Don't blame me. I'm an interpreter. I'm not supposed to know a power _____ from a computer terminal."

JEDI MASTER BONUS #7

Identify the character who referred to Chewie as a "noisy brute."

JEDI MASTER BONUS #8

Who was accused of "having delusions of grandeur"?

42. (Fill in the Blank) Seeing that Leia was angry at him, Han adopted a sarcastic tone. "Well, don't get all _____ on me. So long, Princess."

43. Identify the Rebel who complained that with all the meteor activity in the Hoth system, it was "going to be difficult to spot approaching ships"?
    A. General Rieekan
    B. Princess Leia
    C. Luke Skywalker

44. (Fill in the Blank) After a familiar stream of protesting beeps and whistles from R2-D2, his counterpart replied, "Don't try to blame me. I didn't ask you to turn on the _____ heater. I merely commented that it was freezing in the princess' chamber. But it's supposed to be freezing."

45. What was the Rebel deck officer's reply at Echo Base when Han asked if he knew where Commander Skywalker was?
    A. "I haven't seen him, sir. I assume he is still outside."
    B. "I haven't seen him. It's possible he came in through the south entrance."
    C. "Nobody knows where he is, sir. He doesn't answer his communicator."

46. What was Han's response to the same deck officer after he told Solo, "Your Tauntaun'll freeze before you reach the first marker"?
    A. "Show some faith, son."
    B. "Then I'll see you in hell."
    C. "Just open the damn door."

47. Upon Luke's rescue by Han from the frozen tundra of the Hoth planet, who said, "good to see you fully functional again"?

48. (Fill in the Blank) After Leia informed Han that General Rieekan thought it was dangerous for him to leave the Hoth system until the energy shield was activated, Solo replied, "That's a good story. I think you just can't bear to let a _____ guy like me out of your sight."

49. (True or False) In addition to "laser brain," Leia called Han a "half-witted, scruffy-looking nerf-herder."

50. After an Imperial probe droid was destroyed on the surface of Hoth, which Rebel acknowledged the inevitable, "It's a good bet the Empire knows we're here"?
    A. General Rieekan
    B. Luke Skywalker
    C. Han Solo

51. Identify the Imperial officer who said, "The Hoth system is supposed to be devoid of human forms."

A. Admiral Ozzel
B. Captain Piett
C. General Veers

JEDI MASTER BONUS #9

Who was "as clumsy" as he was "stupid"?

JEDI MASTER BONUS #10

Identify the Rebel pilot assigned to Luke Skywalker's Rogue Squadron who questioned the Rebel base evacuation plan of only "two fighter [escorts] against a Star Destroyer?"

JEDI MASTER BONUS #11

Whose departure briefing advised the Rebel pilots that "the ion cannon will fire several shots to make sure that any enemy ships will be out of your flight path"?

---

52. Who correctly assumed that the Imperial's "primary target" at the Rebel base would be the power generators?
    A. General Rieekan
    B. Princess Leia
    C. Han Solo

53. (Fill in the Blank) Luke ordered his Rogue Squadron to use their "harpoons and _____ cables" and "go for the legs" of the attacking Imperial AT-ATs.

54. Identify the Imperial officer who advised Darth Vader to initiate his landing because he had "reached the main power generator" of the Rebel base on Hoth.

55. Who issued the order, "All troops will debark for ground assault"?

56. Which Rebel leader commanded: "Send all troops in sector twelve to the south slope to protect the fighters" against Imperial attack forces?

57. What was Han's reply after Leia inquired as to why he had not evacuated the Rebel base?
    A. "I heard the command center had been hit."
    B. "I wanted to see you to your transport safely."
    C. "I couldn't leave without saying goodbye, your Worshipfulness."

58. Who told C-3PO to "hurry up" and get aboard the *Millennium Falcon* or the droid was "going to be a permanent resident" of the Rebel base?

59. Who admitted, "I don't know how we're going to get out of this one"?

JEDI MASTER BONUS #12

What was Han Solo's five-word response after C-3PO informed him that the possibility of the *Millennium Falcon* "successfully navigating an asteroid field" was "approximately three thousand, seven hundred and twenty to one"?

---

60. Which character aboard the *Millennium Falcon* believed that the ship and its occupants would be "pulverized" if they remained within the asteroid field?
    A. C-3PO
    B. Han Solo
    C. Princess Leia

61. (Fill in the Blank) As Luke's X-wing approached Dagobah, he reported to R2-D2 that the starfighter's computer scope was "not picking up any cities or _____. Massive life-form readings, though. There's something alive down there . . ."

JEDI MASTER BONUS #13

Based upon Luke's reply, what was R2-D2's "slightly worried question" after the boy reported immense life-form readings were emanating from Dagobah?

---

62. What explanation did Luke give R2-D2 for the bog beast spitting the little droid out of its mouth?
    A. "You must have left it with a bad taste."
    B. "You're lucky you don't taste very good."
    C. "I guess you gave it a bad case of indigestion."

63. Which character wondered if he was "going crazy"?

64. What was Darth Vader's reply after Admiral Piett expressed his concerns about sending Imperial ships into the asteroid field to pursue the *Millennium Falcon?*
    A. "I want that ship, Admiral, not excuses about asteroids."
    B. "Your men and their ships are disposable. I want that ship and its traitors."
    C. "Asteroids do not concern me, Admiral. I want that ship and not excuses."

65. Who was the first to figure out that the asteroid the *Millennium Falcon* landed on was "not entirely stable"?
    A. C-3PO
    B. Chewie
    C. Han Solo

66. (Fill in the Blank) An angry Princess Leia informed Han Solo that "being _____ by you isn't quite enough to get me excited."

67. Who demanded, "Away with your weapon! I mean you no harm"?

68. Before he knew Yoda's true identity, what did Luke tell the little creature he was looking for on Dagobah?
    A. "A great warrior"
    B. "A Jedi Master of great importance"
    C. "A true guardian of justice and freedom"

69. (Fill in the Blank) After "talking" to the *Millennium Falcon*'s computer system in an effort to repair the freighter's hyperdrive, C-3PO complained to Han, "I don't know where your ship learned to communicate, but it has the most peculiar _____."

70. What derogatory name did Leia ask Han to refrain from calling her?

71. What was Han's response after Leia asked him to stop massaging her hands, because they were "dirty"?
    A. "Who cares, Leia. Your heart is clean."
    B. "My hands are dirty, too. What are you afraid of?"
    C. "You've run out of excuses, Leia."

JEDI MASTER BONUS #14

(Fill in the Blank)

C-3PO interrupted Han and Leia's passionate kiss with the announcement, "Sir, sir! I've isolated the _____power flux coupling."

---

72. Identify the Imperial officer who surmised that the *Millennium Falcon* "must have been destroyed" in the asteroid field considering "the amount of damage we've sustained."

73. Who acknowledged that there was "a great disturbance in the Force"?

A. Darth Vader
B. Yoda
C. The Emperor

74. Who did not consider Luke Skywalker a threat to the Empire, calling him "just a boy"?

75. What was Luke's reply when Yoda asked him why he wished to become a Jedi Knight?
    A. "Mostly because of my father, I guess."
    B. "They are great warriors."
    C. "I have always dreamed of becoming one."

76. (True or False) Yoda taught Luke that "a Jedi must have the deepest sense of honor, the most serious intentions."

77. According to Yoda, what two things did a Jedi not "crave"?
    A. "Adventure . . . excitement"
    B. "Danger . . . thrills"
    C. "Revenge . . . retribution"

78. What was Yoda's prediction when Luke told the Jedi Master that he was "not afraid"?
    A. "You will encounter the dark side and it will frighten you."
    B. "Oh, you will be. You will be."
    C. "Wait until you meet those strong in the dark side of the Force."

JEDI MASTER BONUS #15

According to Master Yoda, what three emotions were typical in those strong in the dark side of the Force?

JEDI MASTER BONUS #16

(Fill in the Blank)

As part of Luke's Jedi training, Yoda warned his new student that "once you start down the dark path, forever will it _____ your destiny, consume you it will, as it did Obi-Wan's apprentice."

JEDI MASTER BONUS #17

What was Yoda's answer when Luke asked him what was inside the huge, darkly tangled tree?

---

79. Who told C-3PO to "shut up" when he began to quote "the odds of surviving a direct assault on an Imperial Star Destroyer"?

80. Identify the Imperial officer who assumed "full responsibility for losing" the *Millennium Falcon* during pursuit of the Rebel ship?

81. What was Yoda's explanation for Luke's failure to grasp the full power of the Force?

82. Who lectured Han Solo, ". . . this time you have gone too far" when he piloted the *Millennium Falcon* directly toward the Imperial Star Destroyer, *Avenger?*

83. Who referred to the *Millennium Falcon* as "the fastest hunk of junk in the galaxy"?
     A. Han Solo
     B. Princess Leia
     C. Lando Calrissian

84. What did Lando Calrissian consider "the price you pay for being successful"?

85. What was the "promise" Luke made to Yoda before departing for Bespin's Cloud City?

86. Who warned Luke, "If you choose to face Vader, you will do it alone"?

87. (Fill in the Blank) Yoda's parting advice to Luke was "Strong is Vader. Mind what you have _____. Save you it can."

88. Who complained to Darth Vader after hearing Han Solo's screams filter through the torture room door, "He's no good to me dead"?

89. Identify the character who sarcastically referred to Lando Calrissian as "a real hero"?

90. Who called Cloud City "crude" but "adequate"?

JEDI MASTER BONUS #18

Who deduced that they were "the bait" for Darth Vader's "trap" for Luke on Bespin's Cloud City facility?

JEDI MASTER BONUS #19

Who apologized for Chewie's violent behavior by stating, "After all, he's only a Wookiee"?

THE NITPICKER'S GUIDE:
The Empire Strikes Back

On-camera bloopers, continuity problems, inconsistencies and reversed images remain forever on film in the second installment of the Star Wars *trilogy.*

We've Heard of Faster Than a Speeding Bullet, But This is Really Fast!

During the scene in which a Star Destroyer-led Imperial fleet clears a path through the asteroid field with a barrage of firepower in search of the *Millennium Falcon,* the first asteroid actually begins to explode one or two frames before the Destroyer's laser blast actually strikes it.

Read My Lips

Princess Leia snaps at Han when a tremor from the space slug throws her into his arms, "Captain, being held by you is hardly enough to get me excited." Look closely at Solo's lips and you will see that he's mouthing her dialogue at the same time. Carrie Fisher, who later admitted to using drugs during the movie's filming, had probably forgotten her line and was getting a little help from her costar.

Don't Let It Go to Your Head

When Chewie enters the Cloud City "junk" room to collect the dis-membered remains of C-3PO, a reflection of the camera and several of the crew can be seen in the close-up of the droid's head on the conveyor belt.

More Moves Than Chess Pieces

Lando Calrissian and Han constantly switch sides from one shot to the next during the scene when the Cloud City administrator escorts them down the corridors for "refreshment" in the dining room. In one shot, Solo is on Leia's right with Lando on her left, but in the next shot, the two men have flip-flopped positions. During the remainder of the scene Han remains on the princess' left.

Someone Gave Luke a Hand

Just before Luke drops out of the bottom of the Cloud City air shaft after his climactic lightsaber duel with Darth Vader, you can catch a quick glimpse of the boy with his right hand still attached, although it was sliced off only moments before by his father.

Spare the Rod

During the seconds just before Darth Vader powers on his lightsaber for the first time in Cloud City, you can distinctly see the actual uncolored rod. However, it isn't white as it was in *Star Wars: A New Hope,* but dark gray, which blends in against Vader's black costume and the dark lighting of the Bespin carbon freezing chamber. (Note: The rod of the lightsaber is aimed almost directly at the camera to show the least possible surface area.)

They Don't Call Him Skywalker for Nothing

After Luke knocks Vader off the edge and jumps down behind him during their lightsaber duel, you can hear him land and then bounce upward on a trampolinelike device. Then, for a brief moment, Luke's head reappears at the bottom of the screen.

More Magic Tricks

As Darth Vader uses the dark side of the Force to mentally hurtle boxes and objects at Luke (who is deflecting them with his lightsaber) during their one-on-one battle aboard Cloud City, one of the pieces breaks the window into the immense shaft, and Luke is sucked through. In the next shot, we see him dangling precariously from a catwalk with both hands, and we can only assume that Luke lost his saber when he was abruptly pulled into the void (we seriously doubt he had time to holster the weapon). Yet, in the following sequence he is shown holding his lightsaber again. (Note: This inconsistency is in actuality a direct result of the conversion from film to home video with its modified form of chopped sides. In the letterbox edition, the saber is near the edge of the screen, lying on the catwalk.)

Fashion Statement

During the scene in which Darth Vader asks Admiral Piett, "Did your men disable the *Millennium Falcon*'s hyperdrive?" the Imperial officer's rank insignia switches from the left side of his uniform to the right.

Head Job

When our Rebel heroes are on Bespin's Cloud City, watch for the scene in which the stormtroopers return Han to his cell with Chewie and C-3PO. When the Imperial soldiers drop Han on the floor, keep an eye on the helmet of the stormtrooper on the right. It appears that Solo's arm gets caught momentarily under the trooper's helmet and lifts it just a little off his head. As the soldier exits the cell, you can see that his helmet is slightly askew.

If At First You Don't Succeed . . .

When the Rebel officer gives the order to close the base's shield doors on Hoth, you can see them begin to shut over Chewie's shoulder, but no sound is emitted. The camera cuts to wider shot of Chewie and the doors, and this time they are motionless. Then the shield doors begin to close *for a second time,* but at least they finally produce the desired sound effects.

Bull's-Eye

When Chewie takes cover around the corner of a corridor on Cloud City, the first of two shots hits the wall and leaves a scorched hole. The second weapon's blast comes only seconds after the first and strikes exactly the same charred spot on the wall.

Another Bull's-Eye

During their lightsaber duel on the catwalk above the shaft on Cloud City, Darth Vader's fierce charge forces Luke backward. Swinging violently at the boy, the Dark Lord slices through a railing and creates a light show of electric discharge. If you pay close attention, you can see the remnants of black tape, which more than likely secured some sort of pyrotechnic device at the exact spot where Vader struck the railing and caused the wild display of sparks.

Maybe It Was Armed with a Remote-Controlled Detonation Device

During the pursuit of the *Millennium Falcon* by Imperial forces through the asteroid field, the camera angle cuts to a wide shot. Something very clearly detonates on the surface of one of the asteroids (it even makes the appropriate sound), but nothing is shown striking it. There are two TIE starfighters chasing the *Falcon* at this point; but both ships are visible, and neither of them is the cause of the explosion. More than likely, however, there was originally more film footage shot for the scene, and the real cause of the detonation ended up on the editing room floor.

What Size of Boots Does a Wookiee Wear?

During a scene on Cloud City, when Chewie is running away from the camera, the angle is such that you can see the bottoms of the Wookiee's feet. What is visible, however, is the heel and sole of the boots of Peter Mayhew's costume.

Stealth Lightsaber

During Luke and Vader's climactic battle on the Cloud City catwalk, just after the Dark Lord says ". . . don't make me destroy you" and before the line of dialogue ". . . you do not yet realize your importance . . ." the scene switches between a shot of Vader from the torso up, to a shot of Luke from over his father's shoulder. Note that Vader's lightsaber has been activated until this point, but now it has mysteriously been turned off. The weapon does not make the characteristic sound of a lightsaber being retracted, and in fact, you can even hear the hum of Vader's weapon until the camera angle changes. Then the sound abruptly disappears.

They Don't Make Droids Like They Used To

When C-3PO walks in on Han and Leia kissing and lifts his arm to tap Solo's shoulder, the "hydraulic mechanism" attached to his elbow and upper arm becomes detached. If you look closely, you can catch a glimpse of it falling to the floor. Then miraculously the "mechanism" appears protruding out of the droid's upper arm, no longer attached to his elbow.

APPEARANCES CAN BE DECEIVING: JEDI MASTER YODA
Imperial Security Bureau (ISB) Dossier #WLD-938

1. (Fill in the blank with the correct number) Yoda was a powerful Jedi Knight who eventually evolved into a Jedi Master of extreme power and ability. For _____ hundred years, this small, elfish, green-skinned being served as a mentor and teacher, training young Jedi in the use of the Force.

2. On what swamp planet did Yoda live in seclusion in an effort to survive the complete eradication of the Jedi Knights by Darth Vader and the Emperor?

3. How old was Yoda when he finally died?

4. What kind of edible swamp stick was the Jedi Master fond of chewing?
    A. Rycrit
    B. Gimer
    C. Jaina

JEDI MASTER BONUS #1

Yoda lectured Luke that "for the Jedi it is time to eat as well." What did he cook in a pot for Luke that the impatient boy found pleasantly surprising?

---

5. (Fill in the blank dialogue) "_____ not make one great" was one of the first pearls of wisdom that Yoda passed on to his new student in his strange dialect.

6. What object did the Jedi Master grab from Luke's supply case?

7. What was Yoda's comment after he took a bite from Luke's food container and then spit it out?

8. How did Yoda describe his imminent death?

9. Before he demanded that Luke use the Force to raise his X-wing starfighter from the murky depths of the swamp, what did Yoda have Luke manipulate as practice tools?

JEDI MASTER BONUS #2

What was the Jedi Master's three-word reply after a panting Luke told him that he could not raise the fighter from the swamp because it was "too big"?

---

10. With his final breath, what did Yoda warn his last student, Luke Skywalker, not to underestimate?

11. Identify the alien species of which Yoda was a member.

12. Although Yoda informed Luke that his training was complete, what did the Jedi Master say would be the boy's ultimate test?

THE EVIL EMPIRE

Supported by an immense war machine and held together by the Emperor's use of the dark side of the Force, the evil Galactic Empire ruled the galaxy for many years. Essentially, the military was the government of the Empire, and those who distinguished themselves during the Galactic Civil War with the Rebellion were rewarded with important command positions or governorships over entire star systems. Who were these loyal, strong-willed and ambitious Imperial officers?

---

1. What was Imperial governor Tarkin's title?

2. When Tarkin announced that the Imperial Senate had been suspended, who did he say would maintain control at the regional level?
   A. The Regional Committees
   B. Outer Rim Administrators
   C. The local governors

3. Which senior officer serving under Tarkin on the original Death Star was in charge of day-to-day monitoring of all systems functions and defensive armament?
   A. General Veers
   B. General Tagge
   C. Admiral Ozzel

4. Who was the commander of the ground troops during the Imperial assault on the Rebel's base during the Battle of Hoth?

5. Darth Vader called Admiral Ozzel clumsy as well as stupid before killing him. What had Ozzel done?

6. Identify the first officer on Vader's flagship *Executor* promoted to admiral and given command of the flagship after Ozzel's untimely demise.
   A. Captain Piett
   B. Captain Brandei
   C. Captain Needa

JEDI MASTER BONUS #1

What was the primary unit used to gauge time throughout the Empire?

---

7. Who was the senior Imperial commander in charge of operations aboard the original Death Star?

8. Identify the elite unit of red-robed soldiers who served as the Emperor's personal protectors.

9. What was the comm-unit designation for the Imperial stormtrooper who left his post while guarding the *Millennium Falcon* on the Death Star?
   A. GB-486
   B. TK-421
   C. JH-225

10. When his aide suggested they needed to escape prior to the destruction of the Death Star, who snapped, "Evacuate? In our moment of triumph? I think you overestimate their chances"?

11. Who did Darth Vader attack in the conference room on the Death Star by using the dark side of the Force?
    A. Admiral Ozzel
    B. Admiral Motti
    C. General Tagge

12. Who suggested the destruction of Alderaan as a demonstration of the Death Star's annihilative capabilities?

JEDI MASTER BONUS #2

Besides Darth Vader, which Imperials were mentioned in *The Empire Strikes Back?*

---

13. How did Grand Moff Tarkin die?

14. What was the unofficial name of Darth Vader's task force during the events leading up to *The Empire Strikes Back's* Hoth battle?
    A. Imperial Annihilation Group
    B. Imperial Death Squadron
    C. Lord Vader's Executor Force

15. (True or False) Vader's task force was comprised of the Dark Lord's flagship *Executor* and six Imperial Star Destroyers.

16. Name the Imperial officer who died a quick, but painful, death because he allowed the *Millennium Falcon* to escape after leaving the asteroid field.

17. Who personally supervised the second Death Star's final stages of construction?

18. (Fill in the Blank) Before Darth Vader punished him for his gross incompetence, Captain Needa had been in command of the _____, an *Imperial*-class Star Destroyer.

JEDI MASTER BONUS #3

Who was Grand Moff Tarkin's adjutant aboard the original Death Star?

---

19. Who named the Emperor's tyrannical and evil regime the Galactic Empire?

20. Why was the Endor star system chosen as the secret construction site for the second Imperial Death Star battle station?

21. In which sector of the Rebel base on Hoth did the Imperial fleet come out of hyperspace?
    A. Sector 69-0
    B. Sector 7
    C. Sector 4

22. Identify the Imperial administrator responsible for governing a large segment of the Outer Rim Territories.

23. Which Imperial aristocrat and soldier commanded the task force accountable for the systematic extermination of all Rebels and their sympathizers on the planet Ralltiir?
    A. Lord Lorrdian
    B. Sir Nergon
    C. Lord Tion

24. Who was the Imperial commander in charge of supervising the construction of the second Death Star in the Endor system?
    A. Moff Jerjerrod
    B. Admiral Nadon
    C. General Moltaak

JEDI MASTER BONUS #4

Name the Imperial officer who was the chief gunnery officer aboard the Star Destroyer *Devastator* when it captured Princess Leia's Rebel Blockade Runner, *Tantive IV*.

---

25. (True or False) Syotate Paotune was the Emperor's Grand Vizier.

26. Identify the military genius who devised and executed the construction of the first Imperial Death Star battle station.
    A. Darth Vader
    B. Grand Moff Tarkin
    C. Admiral Motti

27. What color was the two-piece body glove that Imperial stormtroopers wore underneath their armored spacesuits?

28. What was another name for the exceptionally motivated and specially trained Imperial desert stormtrooper?
    A. Deserttrooper
    B. Sandtrooper
    C. Sandsoldier

29. Identify the three Imperial officers who formed the original Death Star's command triumvirate.

30. Who formulated the infamous doctrine of rule through fear, which the Emperor later used as the foundation for his New Order regime of domination and despotism?

JEDI MASTER BONUS #5

How many pieces made up the outer shell of an Imperial stormtrooper's armored spacesuit?

JEDI MASTER BONUS #6

Name the Imperial space traffic controller aboard the *Executor* Star Destroyer who was in charge of directing interstellar transit within the restricted area surrounding Endor's moon.

MASTER OF THE DARK SIDE: EMPEROR PALPATINE

Bothan Spy Network (BSN) Dossier #42922-5860

NOTE: Because of the difficulty of the following questions, each correct answer will count as a 5-point JEDI MASTER BONUS.

JEDI MASTER BONUS #1

Identify the elected office in the Old Republic's galactic government that Senator Palpatine held prior to declaring himself Emperor of the New Order.

JEDI MASTER BONUS #2

Name the Old Republic's senior Senator, regarded as the Emperor's oldest enemy.

JEDI MASTER BONUS #3

Who formed the Alliance to Restore the Republic in an effort to thwart the Emperor's galaxy-wide rule of tyranny?

JEDI MASTER BONUS #4

(Fill in the blank dialogue)

Emperor Palpatine disbanded the Imperial Senate "for the duration of the _____ only."

JEDI MASTER BONUS #5

(Fill in the blank dialogue)

Grand Moff Tarkin announced to the military command aboard the original Death Star battle station, "The Imperial Senate will no longer be of any concern to us. I've just received word that the Emperor has dissolved the council permanently. The last _____ of the Old Republic have been swept away."

JEDI MASTER BONUS #6

From where in the second Death Star did the Emperor oversee the aerial Battle of Endor?

JEDI MASTER BONUS #7

What was the Emperor's three-word response after Darth Vader informed his master that "a small Rebel force has penetrated the shield and landed on Endor"?

JEDI MASTER BONUS #8

What "feelings" did the Emperor urge Luke Skywalker to use in an effort to convert the boy to the dark side of the Force?

JEDI MASTER BONUS #9

What were Emperor Palpatine's final words before Darth Vader threw him to his death?

GAMBLER'S LUCK: THE LOWDOWN ON LANDO CALRISSIAN

Imperial Security Bureau (ISB) Dossier #YIH-216

1. What was Lando's "respectable" title at the Tibanna-gas mining operation on Bespin's Cloud City?
   A. Chief Operating Officer
   B. Baron-Administrator
   C. On-site Operations Manager

2. Always the master gambler, how did Lando win stewardship of the floating metropolis?

3. Although Lando didn't have "any love for the Empire," Darth Vader made the one-time interstellar con man an offer that he couldn't refuse. What was it?

4. Prior to joining the Rebel Alliance against the Empire, in what small but significant military conflict did Lando participate?
   A. The Two Day War of Virgilio
   B. The Battle of Taanab
   C. The Raid on Ka'taria

5. What was the name of Lando's cyborg aide on Cloud City?

JEDI MASTER BONUS #1

Identify the code Lando used to covertly order the Cloud City guards to capture the Imperial stormtroopers.

6. What did Han Solo do to Lando when the Cloud City administrator tried to make excuses for his betrayal?

7. Who called Lando an "old smoothie"?

8. (Fill in the blank dialogue) When Han asked Lando if the Cloud City gas mine was "paying off," his old friend and sometime-rival answered, "We're a small outpost and not very self-sufficient. And I've had _____ problems of every kind. I've had labor difficulties . . ."

9. Why was Lando afraid of the Empire?

10. How did Lando describe Han's condition after he was encased in carbonite by Darth Vader?

11. Who tried to choke Lando?

12. After saving Han and assisting in the destruction of Jabba the Hutt's criminal organization, Lando accepted a military commission in the Rebel Alliance. What rank was he given?

JEDI MASTER BONUS #2

Lando decided to aid the inhabitants of the agrarian Taanab world against marauding pirates because the invaders had damaged his ship and because he felt that they were taking advantage of defenseless farmers. Identify the homeworld of the raiding pirates.

13. What was Lando's pivotal role during the Battle of Endor?

14. Who was Lando's copilot aboard the *Millennium Falcon* during the decisive Galactic Civil War battle?

15. Name the veteran X-wing pilot who accompanied Lando on the run to destroy the second Death Star's power core.

JEDI MASTER BONUS #3

What type of sublight-speed projectiles did Lando fire at the Death Star's main reactor, effectively penetrating and destroying the Imperial battle station?

BEHIND-THE-SCENES
Return of the Jedi

1. Identify the director first approached by George Lucas to helm the third and final installment of the *Star Wars* trilogy?
   A. Richard Marquand
   B. Irvin Kershner
   C. Francis Ford Coppola

2. How many puppeteers (using both hands) operated the Jabba the Hutt creature?
   A. Five
   B. Ten
   C. Twelve

3. Which major character was originally scripted to perish in the Death Star explosion, but was given a second chance at cinematic life after a poor preview audience reception?

4. (True or False) Experiments with a computer to generate a random but logical language for some of the movie's creatures produced a dialect of Japanese.

5. Portions of the partially completed Death Star model resembled which city's skyline?
   A. New York
   B. Paris
   C. San Francisco

6. The official reason for the film's title change from *Revenge of the Jedi* to *Return of the Jedi* was that "... a Jedi would not take revenge." In reality, why was the original title leaked early in production?

JEDI MASTER BONUS #1

Name the three actors who participated in the portrayal of the Darth Vader character in *Return of the Jedi*.

---

7. As an "inside joke," what did members of the special effects crew insert into a tremendously complex dogfight sequence between Imperial and Rebel spacecraft?
    A. A ship that looked *very* similar to *Star Trek's* U.S.S. Enterprise
    B. A tennis shoe
    C. A *Mars* candy bar

8. What was visible on Carrie Fisher's back in the Tatooine desert scene in which a scantily clad Leia turned away from the camera to swing around a mounted laser gun?

9. Whose idea was it to have Princess Leia barely dressed in a skimpy slave girl outfit and serving the loathsome Jabba the Hutt?
    A. George Lucas
    B. Carrie Fisher
    C. Richard Marquand

10. What was the name of the horror movie the producers claimed to be making to preserve secrecy while filming the Jabba the Hutt/sail barge scenes in Yuma, Arizona?
    A. *Murdercycle*
    B. *Making a Killing*
    C. *Blue Harvest*

11. Identify the one Academy Award *Return of the Jedi* won.

12. The Ewoks' home on the Sanctuary Moon of Endor was created and filmed amidst redwood forests near which California city?
    A. Sacramento
    B. Lake Tahoe
    C. Crescent City

13. How many models were used by the special effects technicians in *Return of the Jedi?*
    A. Less than 100
    B. A little more than 100
    C. Over 150

JEDI MASTER BONUS #2

What was the name origin of the skiff guards and hired muscle Klaatu, Barada, and Nikto in crime lord Jabba the Hutt's entourage?

---

14. Lucas used several linguists to create languages for the alien creatures in the movie. The one that the jowled, mouse-eyed Nien Nunb spoke was based off a Kenyan dialect. By accident or by design, what was the literal translation of one of his lines?
    A. "One thousand herds of elephants are standing on my foot."
    B. "May the fleas of a thousand camels infest your armpits."
    C. "The enemy will be buried in mounds of elephant manure."

15. During the battle between the Rebel strike force, the Ewoks and Imperial forces on Endor's forest moon, Chewie climbed

onto an AT-ST and tossed out the occupants. What was the true identity of one of the men?

    A. George Lucas

    B. Director Richard Marquand

    C. Composer John Williams

16. What caused the sluglike black spots to appear on the Emperor's face during the scene in which Luke Skywalker is watching the Rebel fleet being led into a trap from aboard the Death Star battle station?

17. What was the name origin of Ree-Yees, one of the more repulsive of Jabba the Hutt's courtiers?

18. According to the movie's sound effects designer, Ben Burtt, what was the source of the engine sounds for the *Millennium Falcon?*

    A. A recording from the inside of a Grand Prix race car

    B. A recording of a P51 Mustang World War II from an air show

    C. A recording of a Boeing 747 taking off at a LAX airport

19. Which creature was the first to be designed for the movie?

    A. Rancor

    B. Jabba the Hutt

    C. The toadlike Worrt creature outside of Jabba's palace

JEDI MASTER BONUS #3

Identify the scene that had to be cut from the final print of the movie because sand continually gummed up the cameras.

---

20. (Fill in the blank with the correct number) Creature design supervisor Phil Tippett and his crew set up an entire creature bay

and were developing the exotic-looking alien beings _____ months before the script was finalized.

21. (True or False) The Ewok actors stormed off the set during filming, but returned with the entire group all wearing *Revenge of the Ewoks* T-shirts.

22. (Fill in the Blank) One of the songs that the Ewoks sang in the movie was Swedish for "It smells of _____ here."

23. What was used by sound effects designer Ben Burtt to produce the "throbbing" noise aboard several of the large spaceships in the movie?
    A. A construction site jackhammer
    B. An amplified heart beat
    C. A malfunctioning motel air conditioner

24. Which alien language was considered the "biggest challenge" to the film's sound effects design technicians?
    A. Jabba the Hutt's
    B. The Ewoks'
    C. Bib Fortuna's

25. Which ending was originally shot and then later discarded before the final print of *Return of the Jedi* was released?
    A. The long-awaited marriage between Leia and Han
    B. A conversation between Luke and the spirit forms of his father, Ben Kenobi and Yoda
    C. A passionate kiss between Leia and Han while the Ewoks applauded

26. (True or False) The name "Ewok" is never used to refer to the teddy bear-like creatures in the movie, though it does appear in the credits and production notes.

27. Whose idea was it to place some sort of monster in the pit under Jabba the Hutt's palace court?

JEDI MASTER BONUS #4

Identify the visual effects wizard who sketched the design for the Rancor beast.

---

28. How many puppeteers operated the Rancor rod-puppet?
    A. Two
    B. Three
    C. Six

29. Which actor described his role in the movie as "just like Bob Hope on the Road. Here we are, two men rapidly approaching middle age, acting silly, shooting monsters"?
    A. Harrison Ford
    B. Mark Hamill
    C. Billy Dee Williams

JEDI MASTER BONUS #5

Name the four men who spent six full days in script conferences during the summer of 1981, discussing the characters and their histories, the plot lines, and the answers to the questions raised in the first two *Star Wars* films.

---

30. Which national publication's June 21, 1983, "Star Wars Goes on Vacation" cover showcased Darth Vader with a boom box, a Gamorrean with a beach ball, and an Ewok holding up Princess Leia, who was stretched out on the beach in her barely nothing slave girl outfit?

31. Lucas was determined to keep *Return of the Jedi*'s plot from being revealed prematurely. How many *full* and *complete* scripts actually existed?

A. Three
B. Six
C. Twelve

32. What was the biggest set constructed for the movie?

33. How many puppeteers used marionette strings to operate the Sy Snootles creature in Jabba the Hutt's court?

34. (True or False) Three operators were actually hidden inside the Jabba the Hutt creature: one in the tail and two in the front, manipulating the head and the arms.

35. (True or False) One of the posters for *Return of the Jedi*, in which two hands hold aloft a Jedi lightsaber, was drawn from photos of George Lucas holding a lightsaber prop.

36. How many days of filming were canceled due to sandstorms in Yuma, Arizona, when the movie was on location for the desert sequences involving Jabba the Hutt's sail barge?
    A. Two
    B. Four
    C. Six

37. During media interviews to promote *Return of the Jedi*, who referred to C-3PO and R2-D2 as the "Laurel and Hardy in metal"?

JEDI MASTER BONUS #6

How many matte painting effects were produced for the movie?

---

38. Besides the sandstorms, what was the biggest problem the film crew encountered during location filming in Yuma, Arizona?

39. Of all the memorabilia and merchandise generated from the *Star Wars* saga, what is George Lucas' favorite and the only collectible he has retained since *Return of the Jedi* was released?
    A. A battery-operated lightsaber
    B. A stuffed Ewok doll
    C. A Wookiee mug

40. How many Ewok masks and headgear were designed and constructed in England for use in the movie?
    A. Forty
    B. Sixty
    C. Eighty

41. (True or False) Except in the case of the Rancor monster, the film's creature design technicians were working without any previously established drawings or sketches.

42. (Fill in the blank with the correct number) The Rancor puppet was filmed at _____ frames per second instead of the normal 24 frames per second. By shooting at an accelerated speed and slowing the projection down later, the visual effects crew attempted to give the feeling of "solidity and weight to the creature."

43. Who said in interviews promoting *Return of the Jedi*'s release, "There have been a lot of directors and studios who have been misled by the success of *Star Wars* into thinking that special effects are everything. They're not. Special effects have their place—and a very special place—in the *Star Wars* saga. But first and foremost comes the story . . . the story is what really counts"?
    A. George Lucas
    B. Richard Marquand
    C. Mark Hamill

JEDI MASTER BONUS #7

Who publicly criticized director Richard Marquand's decision to show the face of Darth Vader in *Return of the Jedi*, calling it a "cheat" because the audience should have "had to imagine what the face looked like"?

---

44. (True or False) Although there were normally 100–150 people at any given time on the set of a *Star Wars* movie, during a particularly sensitive point in the story development of *Return of the Jedi*, only four or five members of the film crew would be allowed on the set.

45. How long was the film model of Admiral Ackbar's personal flagship, *Home One?*
    A. Eight feet
    B. Ten feet
    C. Sixteen feet

46. Which type of internal lighting did the model makers use to give them a sense of scale?
    A. Halogen
    B. Fluorescent
    C. Neon

47. Why were dwarves used instead of midgets to play the parts of the Ewoks?

48. Body casts had to be designed and constructed for each dwarf's head, arms, chest, legs, and each finger and fingernail, to fit a matching Ewok outfit. Why were the costumes' booties remade at the last minute prior to shooting?

49. (Fill in the blank with the correct number) Building the set that showed the surface of the Death Star battle station, and the

tunnels leading to its interior, meant creating a series of trenches and tunnel sections that were two feet high, four feet wide, and over _____ feet long.
    A. sixty-one
    B. seventy-two
    C. ninety-six

50. Which set was considered by the film crew to be a "nightmare" because of the heat and claustrophobic environment?
    A. The interior of Jabba the Hutt's sail barge
    B. Jabba's court inside his Tatooine palace
    C. The Emperor's throne room aboard the Death Star

51. (True or False) The movie set in Yuma, Arizona, was an enormous project that took eight months to construct, making it one of the largest sets ever built for a film.

52. (True or False) The long search to find a location for the scenes set on the Ewoks' forest moon of Endor began in Santa Cruz, in Southern California, and continued all the way up the West Coast to British Columbia in Canada.

53. What major *Star Wars* actor commented during promotional interviews for *Return of the Jedi*, "I'm the face that nobody knows, your favorite voice"?

54. (True or False) The cameras kept rolling on *Return of the Jedi* for twenty-four hours a day with crews working six days a week.

55. Identify the weekly publication whose May 23, 1983 cover boldly proclaimed, "*Star Wars III, Return of the Jedi:* George Lucas & Friends Wrap It All Up."
    A. *People*
    B. *Time*
    C. *US*

JEDI MASTER BONUS #8

Who publicly defended the film's "weakest of the three" rap by the critics with, ". . . everything that has been set up, you can't bring a trilogy to a conclusion without disappointing some people"?

---

56. (True or False) A sequence was filmed but later cut from the final print in which Luke visited Obi-Wan's house, constructed his new lightsaber, and received a telepathic message from Darth Vader before sending the droids to Jabba the Hutt's palace.

57. (True or False) A 1983 *Star Wars* related television special was called *Space Creatures: Return of the Jedi*.

58. What was the name of the 1985 PBS "making of" TV special?
    A. *From Star Wars to Jedi: The Making of a Saga*
    B. *From Star Wars to Return of the Jedi: The Making of a Space Saga*
    C. *The Making of a Space Opera: Behind-the-Scenes of Return of the Jedi*

59. In 1985 George Lucas attempted to bring *Star Wars* to animated television, using none of the main characters from the films other than C-3PO, R2-D2 and some of the Ewoks. What was the name of the short-lived ABC-TV Saturday morning cartoon series?

60. (True or False) A scene filmed but later cut from *Return of the Jedi*'s released version involved Darth Vader choking two red-robed Imperial Royal Guards who disallowed him access to the Emperor.

61. Prior to the naming of Richard Marquand as director of the film, who was reportedly Lucas' choice to helm the third installment of the *Star Wars* saga?

62. Which two countries had teams of creature makers working simultaneously thousands of miles apart on two different sets of Ewok costumes?

63. For the sequence in which the Ewoks attacked an Imperial AT-ST, the movie's model makers came up with a technique that realistically showed what looked like massive redwood logs crushing the head of an enemy "scout walker." In reality, how large in diameter were the logs?
    A. One foot
    B. Six inches
    C. One inch

64. Why did the use of dwarves as Ewoks require more rehearsal time?

65. Which incredibly detailed spacecraft in *Return of the Jedi* did the model building wizards at ILM consider their "crowning achievement" of the entire *Star Wars* saga?
    A. B-wing Rebel starfighter
    B. The uncompleted Death Star battle station
    C. Imperial shuttle *Tydirium*

JEDI MASTER BONUS #9

What were the titles of the two made-for-TV Ewok movies?

JEDI MASTER BONUS #10

Return of the Jedi: The Special Edition featured an enhanced cabaret sequence in Jabba the Hutt's palace. Identify the internationally popular singer and musician whom George Lucas wanted to write the score for the new scene, but passed.

JEDI MASTER BONUS #11

George Lucas has stated in several interviews that he did not like the Ewok celebration and accompanying music at the end of the original film version. Identify the three planets whose inhabitants were shown in the much more satisfying galaxy-wide celebration at the conclusion of *The Special Edition,* which included musical soundtrack re-scoring by John Williams.

---

66. Identify the actor whose sinister role in *The Maltese Falcon* inspired the debauched Jabba the Hutt character.

67. (Fill in the blank with the correct number) Hidden cables in the full-scale Jabba allowed as many as _____ off-camera puppeteers to operate the various functions that animated the creature.

68. The movie's creature makers gave nicknames to their works in progress. What was Ishi Tib's a.k.a.?
    A. "Droopy Jowls"
    B. "Starfish"
    C. "Nixon"

69. Which actor wanted his character killed off at the beginning of the film as a martyr to the Rebellion?

70. Who originally wanted the Rancor beast to be "the best
    Godzilla that had ever been done"?
    A. Richard Marquand
    B. Phil Tippett
    C. George Lucas

71. How many feet in height was the foam-rubber Rancor rod-
    puppet?
    A. Two
    B. Three
    C. Four

72. (True or False) The sail barge desert scenes, which were filmed
    in Yuma, Arizona, cost two million dollars to produce.

JEDI MASTER BONUS #12

A visually impressive scene in *Return of the Jedi* was when
thousands of Imperial soldiers seemed to assemble in the
Death Star battle station's docking bay, standing at attention to receive the Emperor and his entourage. A matte
painting, however, provided the bulk of the foot soldiers.
In reality, how many costumed extras were used in the
scene?

---

73. (True or False) Originally, the Mon Calamari being, Ackbar,
    was one of many anonymous creatures created for the movie,
    but when Lucas saw the alien creature one day, he "knighted"
    him an admiral in the Rebel Alliance.

74. There were two versions of Admiral Ackbar, one being a slip-
    on head harness that had ancillary cables hidden off camera
    to operate the eyes and mouth. What was used for close-up
    shots?

75. What was the nickname given to one of Jabba the Hutt's skiff
    helmsman, Pote Snitkin, by the movie's creature makers?

A. Snit Plotkin
B. Snake Plissken
C. Potty Snackin'

76. (Fill in the blank with the correct number) The sail barge scene in the Yuma desert was shot on _____ acres surrounded by a chain-link fence with local police and production security patrolling the perimeter.

77. (True or False) The Imperial "walker" models were filmed on a miniature forest set under natural sunlight at ILM's Marin County facility, and as stop-motion puppets.

78. Who wanted to sculpt Neanderthal-like cannibal creatures as the Ewoks, but was vetoed by George Lucas, who envisioned the Endor moon inhabitants as cute and cuddly?

79. In addition to Admiral Ackbar, what other creature creation was snatched out of anonymity to have a supporting role in the movie's climactic Battle of Endor?

80. How many separate effects shots did ILM have to create for *Return of the Jedi?*
    A. 300
    B. 400
    C. 500

JEDI MASTER BONUS #13

What was the tagline of the fake movie production, *Blue Harvest,* which was created to provide cover and security for *Jedi*'s plot development while filming in the Yuma, Arizona, desert?

JEDI MASTER BONUS #14

(Fill in the blank with the correct number) For _____ months prior to filming, the movie's creature makers developed designs of the strange denizens who formed Jabba the Hutt's criminal entourage at his palace on Tatooine.

JEDI MASTER BONUS #15

Identify the actors who provided the voices of Yoda, Darth Vader, Boba Fett, Han Solo, Princess Leia and Jabba the Hutt for the *Return of the Jedi* radio dramatization.

JEDI MASTER BONUS #16

Name the artist who painted the matte effect for the scene in which the Emperor arrived aboard the Death Star battle station, received by thousands of Imperial troops.

JEDI MASTER BONUS #17

(Fill in the blank with the correct number)

A *Star Wars* or *Empire Strikes Back* optical shot typically had thirty to forty separate elements or individual pieces of film. *Return of the Jedi,* however, had shots that required between twenty and eighty elements, with one complex space battle in particular using more than _____ hundred separate elements.

THE NAME GAME
Return of the Jedi

Match the name of the actor with the corresponding character portrayed in the third and final installment of the Star Wars *trilogy.*

1. _____ Dermot Crowley   A. Wicket
2. _____ Jane Busby   B. Bib Fortuna
3. _____ Femi Taylor   C. Admiral Ackbar
4. _____ Kenny Baker   D. Moff Jerjerrod
5. _____ Tim Rose   E. Paploo
6. _____ Mike Edmonds   F. Chief Chirpa
7. _____ Michael Carter   G. Sy Snoodles
8. _____ Annie Arbogast   H. Oola
9. _____ Caroline Blakiston   I. General Madine
10. _____ Warwick Davis   J. Mon Mothma
11. _____ Michael Pennington   K. Logray
12. _____ Jack Purvis   L. Teebo

JEDI MASTER BONUS #1

According to the movie's end credits, she played the Fat Dancer. What is this supporting cast member's name?

JEDI MASTER BONUS #2

Identify the three puppeteers who animated the Jabba the Hutt creature.

JEDI MASTER BONUS #3

Which one of the following was NOT listed in the credits as an Ewok warrior: Nick Morrison, Malcolm Dixon, or Mike Cottrell?

JEDI MASTER BONUS #4

Name the supporting actors who portrayed Star Destroyer Captain No. 1 and No. 2, respectively.

STAR POWER
Part II

1. (True or False) Each S-foil wing section of an X-wing starfighter was joined to the transverse wing section opposite it.

2. Which armor-hulled vehicle in Jabba the Hutt's fleet did the crime lord's associates use to stage raids?

3. When the *Millennium Falcon* was captured by the original Death Star, why did the Imperial forces believe the crew had escaped?

4. (True or False) The Imperial AT-AT walkers destroyed the power generators at Hoth's Echo Base.

5. What part of the *Millennium Falcon* was Chewie working on at the beginning of *The Empire Strikes Back?*
   A. The boosting mechanism of the deflector shields
   B. The weapons system
   C. The central lifters

6. Which character finally repaired the *Falcon*'s hyperdrive at the end of *The Empire Strikes Back?*
   A. Lando Calrissian
   B. R2-D2
   C. Chewie

JEDI MASTER BONUS #1

(Fill in the blank with the correct number)

A skiff utilized repulsors to float and move about the surface terrain, and was operated by a pilot who navigated the vehicle with _____ directional steering vanes.

---

7. (True or False) The cargo capacity of the Empire's second Death Star was over one million kilotons.

8. Where were the maneuver controls located on a speeder bike?
   A. In the handgrips
   B. At the forward end of the saddle seat
   C. In the rocker-pivoted foot pads

9. (Fill in the blank with the correct number) The newest model in the Imperial fleet, the *Super*-class Star Destroyer, was _____ kilometers long.
   A. Seven
   B. Eight
   C. Nine

10. (Fill in the blank dialogue) Han Solo praised Luke Skywalker after the original Death Star was destroyed: "Great shot, kid. That was one in a _____."

11. Which Rebel military starfighter was built to serve as an escort craft for larger starships?
    A. A-wing
    B. X-wing
    C. Y-wing

12. What was the crew complement of the AT-ST's small, armored-plated command pod?

JEDI MASTER BONUS #2

What were the compound names for AT-ATs and AT-STs?

---

13. How many meters in height was an AT-ST?
    A. Five
    B. Six
    C. Seven

14. (True or False) The two secondary airfoils of a B-wing starfighter could vary their position during flight.

15. (Fill in the Blank) A B-wing fighter utilized an automatic gyroscopically stabilized _____ system to maintain the command pod in an immovable position.

16. (True or False) The original Death Star battle station's superlaser could be adjusted to various settings.

17. What Alliance starfighter played an important role in the Rebel's decisive Battle of Endor?

18. How many meters in length was the Y-wing starfighter?
    A. Twelve
    B. Fourteen
    C. Sixteen

JEDI MASTER BONUS #3

What was the exact length of an X-wing starfighter from nose to engine block?

---

19. What was the crew complement of a Y-wing starfighter?

20. What was the crew complement of an X-wing starfighter?

21. Which Rebel Alliance starfighter had an indentation socket positioned on the outer hull behind the cockpit, utilized by an interfacing R2 droid unit?
    A. X-wing
    B. B-wing
    C. A-wing

22. What was the name of the *Lambda*-class Imperial shuttle covertly used by Han Solo's special strike force in an effort to reach the forest moon of Endor and sabotage the shield generator protecting the second Death Star?
    A. *Subjugator*
    B. *Tydirium*
    C. *Scardia*

23. (True or False) Rebel Alliance transport ships were equipped with hyperdrives and bristled with defensive weaponry such as turboblasters and ion cannon batteries.

24. (True or False) A Rebel transport ship's command crew operated out of a small, confining pod positioned toward the rear of the spacecraft and atop the outer hull.

JEDI MASTER BONUS #4

How many ion engines provided the propulsion for deep-space Imperial TIE starfighters?

---

25. (True or False) Some TIE fighters had bent-wing design and double command pods.

26. What was the name of Princess Leia's Blockade Runner, captured by Darth Vader and his Imperial minions at the beginning of *Star Wars: A New Hope?*

    A. *Independence II*
    B. *Tantive IV*
    C. *Defiant III*

27. What were the three classes of Imperial Star Destroyers?
    A. *Imperial, Super* and *Victory*
    B. *Emperor, Marauder* and *Devastator*
    C. *Avenger, Executor* and *Super*

28. What did the Imperial Star Destroyer *Avenger* release before making the jump to hyperspace in *The Empire Strikes Back?*

29. What color were snowspeeders?
    A. White, with dark gray-colored trim
    B. Rust, with light gray-colored trim
    C. Gray, with rust-colored trim

30. What was the main objective of the AT-AT walkers at the Battle of Hoth?

JEDI MASTER BONUS #5

How many AT-AT walkers did the Rebel troops see on the north ridge advancing toward Echo Base?

---

31. (True or False) A jabbering Jawa scurried up to Luke Skywalker's landspeeder and began fondling it as soon as the boy parked the vehicle in front of the Mos Eisley cantina.

32. How did the crew of the *Millennium Falcon* locate the tractor beam on the Death Star in *Star Wars?*

33. Which class of Imperial Star Destroyers was in service at the end of the Clone Wars?

34. Where were the controls for a speeder bike's parking, weaponry, communications and energy recharging located on the small, one-person vehicle?

35. (True or False) The *Millennium Falcon* was approximately thirty-seven meters in length.

36. (True or False) The reconstructed *Falcon* had a more powerful starship engine, armored hull, and weapons system than allowed for a ship of its size and class.

JEDI MASTER BONUS #6

What race of humans designed the *Millennium Falcon?*

---

37. What type of small star cruiser carried medical supplies and facilities for treating the sick and wounded?

38. What was the maximum passenger complement of Imperial *Lambda*-class shuttles?
    A. Twenty
    B. Twenty-five
    C. Thirty-six

39. (True or False) Passengers and crew members of a *Lambda*-class shuttle entered and exited the craft through a side hatch which dropped open upon landing.

40. (Fill in the Blank) Escape pods utilized _____ distress beacons and were designed to float through space like buoys until a ship picked up the signal and came to their rescue.

41. (True or False) Cloud cars, such as the ones in use outside of Bespin's Cloud City mining colony and trading outpost, employed both repulsorlifts and ion engines.

42. (True or False) Rebel Alliance X-wing starfighters were also equipped with starship engines and interrelated systems for propulsion to supralight speeds.

43. (Fill in the blank with the correct number) Imperial speeder bike scouts were ordered to make continuous sensor scans and report in every _____ minutes.

JEDI MASTER BONUS #7

How many kilometers in diameter was the original Imperial Death Star?

JEDI MASTER BONUS #8

From bow to stern, how many meters in length was Boba Fett's starfighter, *Slave I*, and what was its class?

JEDI MASTER BONUS #9

(Fill in the blank with the correct number)

Darth Vader's *Super*-class Star Destroyer, *Executor*, was five times larger than the *Imperial*-class, measuring _____ meters in overall length.

REBEL RUMBLINGS & IMPERIAL TRANSMISSIONS
Return of the Jedi

1. What was Darth Vader's response when Commander Jerjerrod informed the Dark Lord, "I assure you . . . my men are working as fast as they can" to complete the Death Star as scheduled?
    A. "Perhaps they need some incentive from me to make this station fully operational."
    B. "For your sake, you better hope that is a correct appraisal of the situation."
    C. "Perhaps I can find new ways to motivate them."

2. What did Jabba the Hutt consider his "favorite decoration" in his desert palace on Tatooine?

3. Who did the crime lord refer to as "fearless and inventive"?

4. (Fill in the Blank) An angry Jabba told Han Solo after Leia decarbonized him, "You may have been a good smuggler, but now you're _____ fodder."

5. Who warned Luke, "Do not underestimate the powers of the Emperor"?
    A. Obi-Wan Kenobi
    B. Darth Vader
    C. Yoda

6. Identify the recipient of Luke's agonizing confession, "I can't do it . . . I can't go on alone" after Yoda's passing on Dagobah.

JEDI MASTER BONUS #1

(Fill in the Blank)

As part of his final training as a Jedi, Obi-Wan instructed Luke, ". . . you must confront and then go beyond the dark side—the side your father couldn't get past. Impatience is the easiest door—for you, like your father. . . . You're no longer so _____ now, Luke. You are strong and patient. And now you must face Darth Vader again!"

---

7. (Fill in the Blank) When Luke told his father, "I feel the conflict within you. Let go of your hate," Vader replied matter-of-factly, "It is too late for me, son. The Emperor will show you the true _____ of the Force. He is your master now."

8. Who was Leia referring to when she said to Han, "I'm afraid our furry companion has gone and done something rather rash"?
    A. Paploo
    B. Chewie
    C. Wicket

9. Of the three—Luke, Vader and the Emperor—who made the observation, "Your overconfidence is your weakness"?
    A. The Emperor
    B. Vader
    C. Luke

10. Identify the Rebel who issued the order to the other X-wing starfighter pilots, "Lock S-foils in attack positions" during the armada's assault on the Death Star.

    A. Green Leader
    B. Red Leader
    C. Gray Leader

11. (True or False) After C-3PO announced that Jabba the Hutt would take pleas for mercy, Han arrogantly stepped forward on the skiff plank above the Sarlacc pit and shot back, ". . . you tell that slimy piece of . . . worm-ridden filth he'll get no such pleasure from us."

12. Which one of Jabba's motley array of intergalactic sidekicks did C-3PO call a "beast"?

13. What did Yoda consider "unexpected" and "unfortunate"?

JEDI MASTER BONUS #2

What were Yoda's six and final words to Luke before dying?

JEDI MASTER BONUS #3

(Fill in the blank with the correct number)

A Mon Calamari controller turned away from his screen during the Rebel assault on the second Death Star and called out excitedly to Ackbar, "We have enemy ships in sector _____."

---

14. Who warned Luke, "You cannot escape your destiny"?
    A. The Emperor
    B. Darth Vader
    C. Obi-Wan Kenobi

15. (Fill in the Blank) While on Endor's moon, C-3PO informed Han that it was a violation of his "programming to impersonate a _____."

16. Who readily admitted, "I have a *really* bad feeling about this"?
    A. Han
    B. Leia
    C. Luke

17. (Fill in the Blank) While Wicket clung to Han's leg, he chuckled, "Well, _____ help is better than no help at all . . ."

18. Who referred to C-3PO as "an old friend of mine"?

19. Which Ewok did Han call a "little fur ball"?
    A. Wicket
    B. Paploo
    C. Logray

20. Who told Luke that it was "pointless to resist" the dark side? Darth Vader or the Emperor?

JEDI MASTER BONUS #4

(Fill in the Blanks)

An angry Emperor boasted to Luke, "Everything that has transpired has done so according to my design. Your friends up there on Sanctuary Moon are walking into a trap. As is your Rebel fleet! It was I who allowed the Alliance to know the location of the shield generator. It is quite safe from your pitiful little _____. An entire _____ of my best troops awaits them."

---

21. Whom did Darth Vader warn, "The Emperor is not as forgiving as I am"?
    A. Luke Skywalker
    B. Admiral Piett
    C. Commander Jerjerrod

22. Who said nervously, "I really don't think we should rush into all this"?
    A. Han Solo
    B. C-3PO
    C. Wedge Antilles

23. What was Bib Fortuna's reply to C-3PO after the droid told him, "We—we bring a message to your master, Jabba the Hutt . . . and a gift"?
    A. "Nee Jabba no badda. Me chaade su goodie"
    B. "Nudd Chaa"
    C. "Die Wanna Wanga"

24. After C-3PO initiated one of his typically long dissertations, who snapped back, "Yes or no will do"?

25. Who complained that R2-D2 was "a fiesty little" droid?

26. Identify the language in which Boushh (in reality a disguised Leia) announced to Jabba the Hutt, "I have come for the bounty on this Wookiee."

JEDI MASTER BONUS #5

What was Jabba's two-word reply after C-3PO was granted an audience before the bloated gangster and the droid greeted him with "Good morning"?

---

27. (True or False) R2-D2 projected to Jabba the Hutt and his criminal entourage a ten-foot-tall hologram of Luke Skywalker, who hinted at a possibly "unpleasant confrontation" if a "mutually beneficial . . . arrangement" for Han Solo's release could not be worked out.

28. What was Yoda referring to when he told Luke on Dagobah that, after nine hundred years, he had "earned it"?

29. (Fill in the Blank) When Luke begged the Jedi Master not to die, an obviously sick Yoda replied metaphorically, "_____ is upon me and soon night must fall."

30. Who told Luke that "there is no avoiding the battle"?
    A. Darth Vader
    B. Yoda
    C. Obi-Wan

31. Who called Lando "respectable" and "a fair pilot"?

32. Identify the Rebel leader who announced, "The Emperor has made a critical error and the time for our attack has come"?
    A. Admiral Ackbar
    B. General Madine
    C. Mon Mothma

33. Who proudly proclaimed the *Millennium Falcon* as "the fastest ship in the [Rebel] fleet"?
    A. Han
    B. Lando
    C. Leia

34. What ship was Han referring to when he called it a "piece of junk"?

JEDI MASTER BONUS #6

Who described the moon of Endor as "pretty"?

JEDI MASTER BONUS #7

(Fill in the Blank)

After Darth Vader informed the Emperor that he "felt" Luke's presence with the Rebel strike force on Endor's moon, the galaxy's Supreme Ruler complained, "Strange that I have not. I wonder if your _____ on this matter are clear, Lord Vader."

---

35. (Fill in the Blank) After Luke took Leia's helmet to where Han had found the charred wreckage of a speeder bike, C-3PO quietly and sadly stated, "I'm afraid that Artoo's _____ can find no trace of Princess Leia."

36. Who did Han accuse of "always thinking with your stomach"?

37. (Fill in the Blank) After the Ewoks captured the Rebel strike force on Endor's moon, Han asked C-3PO, "Why don't you use your _____ influence and get us out of this?"

38. Who was supposed to be the "main course" at an Ewok banquet in C-3PO's honor?
     A. Chewie
     B. Han
     C. Luke

39. (True or False) A worried Han Solo demanded C-3PO to tell the Ewoks that "if they don't do as you wish, you'll become angry and use your magic."

40. Who told Luke to "run away, far away" if Darth Vader could feel his presence on Endor's moon?

JEDI MASTER BONUS #8

According to the Emperor, what had made Luke "powerful" in the Force?

JEDI MASTER BONUS #9

(Fill in the Blank)

The shuttle captain of Darth Vader's short-range personnel transporter contacted the Imperial Death Star and asked for clearance to land aboard the battle station: "Command station, this is ST 321. Code clearance _____. We're starting our approach. Deactivate the security shield."

---

41. Upon meeting Vader, who remarked, ". . . this is an unexpected pleasure"?
    A. Lando Calrissian
    B. Moff Jerjerrod
    C. Admiral Piett

42. Name the Imperial officer who Vader chastised by acknowledging that, "The Emperor does not share your optimistic appraisal of the situation."

43. Where was C-3PO when he confessed to R2-D2 that he had "a bad feeling" about the current situation?
    A. Bespin's Cloud City
    B. Endor's moon
    C. Jabba the Hutt's Tatooine palace

44. Who refused to negotiate by stating, "There will be no bargain"?

45. (Fill in the Blank) The tall, thin droid EV-9D9 informed C-3PO, "We have been without an interpreter since our master got angry with our last protocol droid and _____ him."
    A. disintegrated
    B. dismantled
    C. dismembered

JEDI MASTER BONUS #10

What was the Ubese word that Boushh used to signify acceptance of Jabba's offer of thirty-five thousand for the bounty on Chewbacca?

---

46. What was Boushh/Leia's response when Han asked, "Who are you?"

47. (Fill in the Blank) When an angry Jabba the Hutt discovered that Boushh/Leia had unfrozen Han from the carbonite, Solo attempted to make the gangster one last offer: "Jabba . . . I'll pay you _____! You're throwing away a fortune here. Don't be a fool!"

48. Who issued the warning, "We have powerful friends. You're gonna regret this . . ."?
    A. Leia
    B. Han
    C. C-3PO

49. Who referred to Luke as "crazy" and incapable of even taking "care of himself"?

50. Identify the member of Jabba's criminal entourage whom the crime lord called a "weak-minded fool" in Huttese.

51. (True or False) In a thundering outburst, Jabba the Hutt bellowed to his captives Luke, Han, Chewie and Leia, that they were to "be terminated immediately."

JEDI MASTER BONUS #11

What was Luke's seven-word hypnotic command to Bib Fortuna after they encountered each other in the hallway of Jabba's desert palace?

---

52. Who confessed, "I hate long waits"?

53. (Fill in the Blank) After Darth Vader informed the Emperor that the Death Star would "be completed on schedule," the Dark Lord's master replied, "You have done well . . . and now I sense you wish to continue your _____ for young Skywalker."

54. (True or False) The Emperor boasted to Vader, "Everything is proceeding as I have foreseen"?

55. What was Yoda's response after Luke asked him, ". . . is Darth Vader my father?"
    A. "Your father he is."
    B. "Told you, did he?"
    C. "Mmm . . . rest I need. Yes . . . rest."

56. What was Obi-Wan Kenobi's "certain point of view"?

57. (Fill in the Blank) Obi-Wan philosophized to Luke, ". . . you're going to find that many of the truths we _____ to depend greatly on our own point of view."

58. (Fill in the Blank) Obi-Wan sadly admitted to Luke that his pride had created "terrible _____ for the galaxy."

JEDI MASTER BONUS #12

(Fill in the Blank)

Admiral Ackbar briefed the Rebels prior to the assault on the Death Star: "The shield must be deactivated if any attack is to be attempted. Once the shield is down, our cruisers will create a _____, while the fighters fly into the super-structure and attempt to knock out the main reactor."

59. Which Rebel commanding officer asked Han Solo, "...is your strike team assembled?"
    A. Admiral Ackbar
    B. General Madine
    C. Mon Mothma

60. Who used the word "exciting" to describe the reunion of Luke, Han, Leia, Chewie, Lando and the droids prior to the Battle of Endor?
    A. R2-D2
    B. C-3PO
    C. Chewie

61. Who sadly confessed, "I've got a funny feeling. Like I'm not gonna see her again"?

62. (Fill in the Blank) After the Emperor ordered Vader to "send the fleet to the far side of Endor," the Dark Lord replied, "What of the reports of the Rebel fleet massing near _____?"

63. According to C-3PO, who or what would be responsible for "a new definition of pain and suffering" for our Rebel heroes?

64. What did Luke consider "the last mistake" Jabba would ever make?

65. What was Han's response after Luke told him that there was "nothing to see" on Tatooine?
    A. "You're gonna die here, you know. Convenient."
    B. "How convenient. You were born here and now you're gonna die here."
    C. "I'd prefer to see where I'm gonna die."

JEDI MASTER BONUS #13

(Fill in the Blank)

Translating for Jabba the Hutt, C-3PO announced to Luke and Company across the Tatooine desert via loudspeakers, "Victims of the almighty Sarlacc: His Excellency hopes that you will die _____."

JEDI MASTER BONUS #14

What was Han's two-word reply after Luke boasted, "I've taken care of everything" as they were being led to their deaths by Jabba's henchmen?

---

66. (True or False) Han arrogantly warned Jabba, "This is your last chance. Free us or die."

67. (True or False) During the battle between Luke and Company and Jabba and his criminal associates in the Tatooine desert, Han consoled Lando, "It's all right. Trust me."

68. (Fill in the Blank) Just before he died, the Jedi Master Yoda informed Luke, "No more _____ do you require. Already know you that which you need."

69. Who admitted a possible error in judgment, stating, "... it certainly wouldn't have been for the first time"?

70. Who described Darth Vader as "twisted and evil"?
    A. Yoda
    B. Leia
    C. Obi-Wan

71. What did Obi-Wan say taught Luke "among other things, the value of patience"?

72. What did Obi-Wan warn Luke to bury "deep down" or they would "be made to serve the Emperor"?

73. Who made the promise that the *Millennium Falcon* wouldn't even "get a scratch" during the Battle of Endor?

JEDI MASTER BONUS #15

(Fill in the Blanks)

Attempting to give Luke solace with his words, Obi-Wan told the boy of his sister: "The Organa household was high-born and politically quite powerful in that system. Leia became a princess by virtue of her _____ . . . no one knew she'd been adopted, of course. But it was a _____ without real power, since Alderaan had long been a democracy . . ."

JEDI MASTER BONUS #16

(Fill in the Blank)

During her briefing to the Rebel troops, Mon Mothma confirmed, "With the Imperial Fleet spread throughout the galaxy in a _____ effort to engage us, it is relatively unprotected."

---

74. Who told Darth Vader that his "work" aboard the Death Star was "finished"?

75. Who called one of the Ewoks "a jittery little thing"?
    A. Luke
    B. Leia
    C. Han

76. What did the Emperor predict would be Luke's "undoing" as a Jedi Knight?

77. Who surmised that the Ewoks were speaking in a "very primitive dialect"?

78. What did C-3PO say "wouldn't be proper"?

JEDI MASTER BONUS #17

What two things did Leia tell Luke she remembered about her deceased mother?

---

79. Who did Luke consider the "only hope for the Alliance"?

80. What was Darth Vader's response after Luke called him "father" for the first time?
    A. "So, you have accepted the truth."
    B. "It was wise for you to acknowledge your lineage."
    C. "Now you finally understand your destiny."

81. Who was described as "very beautiful . . . kind, but sad"?

82. What was Vader referring to when he said it ". . . no longer has any meaning for me"?
    A. His past as a Jedi Knight
    B. The name Anakin Skywalker
    C. The light side of the Force

83. Who told Luke that he didn't "know the power of the dark side"?

A. Vader
B. The Emperor
C. Obi-Wan

84. Which member of the Rebel strike force acknowledged, "The main entrance to the control bunker's on the far side of that landing platform. This isn't gonna be easy"?

85. Who told C-3PO about the existence of "a secret entrance" to the Imperial bunker "on the other side of the ridge"?

86. Which Rebel confessed that if Han's strike team wasn't successful in sabotaging the shield generator on time, the Alliance's assault on the Death Star would "be the shortest offensive of all time"?
    A. Han
    B. Leia
    C. Lando

87. Who ruined the Rebel strike force's "surprise attack"?
    A. Wicket
    B. Paploo
    C. Chewie

88. According to Luke, what was the Emperor "gravely mistaken" about?

89. (Fill in the Blank) As the *Millennium Falcon* and several squads of Rebel starfighters engaged an armada of TIE fighters, Lando Calrissian ordered, "Accelerate to _____ speed! Draw their fire away from the cruisers."

90. Which word did the Emperor use to describe the Rebellion?
    A. "insignificant"
    B. "weak"
    C. "inconsequential"

91. What did the Emperor consider "unavoidable"?

JEDI MASTER BONUS #18

Who proclaimed that the Emperor had "something special planned" for the Rebel assault fleet?

JEDI MASTER BONUS #19

As a horrified Luke witnessed the aerial battle fireworks between the Rebel and Imperial ships, the Emperor boasted, "As you can see, my young _____, your friends have failed."

---

92. Who ordered the Rebel armada to "prepare to retreat" when it was tragically obvious that the Death Star was fully operational?
    A. General Madine
    B. Admiral Ackbar
    C. Mon Mothma

93. (Fill in the Blank) As Luke's eyes became full of rage, the Emperor smiled triumphantly and said, "Good. I can feel your anger. I am defenseless. Take your weapon! Strike me down with all your _____, and your journey towards the dark side will be complete."

94. Who lectured Luke, "You are unwise to lower your defenses"? Vader or the Emperor?

95. What was Vader's response after Luke told him, "Your thoughts betray you, Father. I feel the good in you . . . the conflict"?
    A. "You underestimate the power of the dark side."
    B. "There is no conflict."
    C. "Then you are wrong, Luke. Prepare to meet your destiny."

96. (Fill in the Blank) After a controller informed Piett that they'd lost their bridge deflector shield, the Imperial admiral ordered, "Intensify the forward _____. I don't want anything to get through."

JEDI MASTER BONUS #20

The spirit form of Obi-Wan Kenobi consoled a dejected Luke by telling him, "_____ will always be with you."

THE NITPICKER'S GUIDE:
Return of the Jedi

Plot oversights, changed premises, equipment oddities, and continuity and production problems continue with the final installment in the Star Wars *saga.*

You Would Think They'd At Least Look at a Videotape of <u>The Empire Strikes Back</u>

Before Han Solo was lowered into the carbonite freezing chamber toward the end of *The Empire Strikes Back,* he has shackles around the upper half of his torso, which hold his arms next to his body. An Ugnaught removes the shackles, but the harnesslike strap remains. However, when he is unfrozen in *Return of the Jedi,* Solo is no longer restrained by the strap.

Also in the same scenes, Han is not wearing his trademark vest in close-ups, just his white shirt. When the camera cuts to long shots, he is once again wearing the vest. Solo is wearing a tunic-style shirt when he is frozen at Cloud City, but when he is thawed at Jabba's palace he is attired in a double-breasted shirt. One final note: when Han is frozen in the previous movie, his shirt is untucked, but in *Jedi* it is tucked in.

They Probably Didn't Give Him a Raise in Pay, Either

After Piett is promoted from captain to admiral in *The Empire Strikes Back*, his rank insignia is upgraded from three red and blue bars to six. However, throughout the events that occur in *Return of the Jedi*, his insignia is three red and blue bars, even though Piett still holds the rank of admiral.

More Flip-Flops

Watch for the scene in Jabba the Hutt's palace on Tatooine in which the bounty hunter Boushh (Leia in disguise) exposes a thermal detonator. When Boba Fett draws his blaster rifle, note that his rangefinder is on the wrong side of his helmet. Also, the emblems on his armor breastplate are backward, his cape is hanging off his right shoulder (usually it's on the left) and Fett draws with his left hand instead of his right. The entire scene has been "flipped" during the film's postproduction editing.

It's a Good Thing He was Wearing a Helmet

When Lando Calrissian first appears in disguise at Jabba's desert palace, watch closely and you will see that he scrapes his helmet against the low ceiling just before he pulls his mask down to show the audience his true identity. He hits his head hard enough to knock the mask backward for a brief second.

We've Heard That Line Before

When R2-D2 and C-3PO first enter Jabba's throne room, the audience can hear a variety of alien voices in the background. One of the more distinct dialects is the Rodian bounty hunter, Greedo, speaking the *exact* same dialogue he rattled off to Han just before the Corellian smuggler killed him with a blaster in *Star Wars: A New Hope*.

Running Backward

Just after R2-D2 plays Luke's hologram to Jabba and his entourage of fawning criminal associates, the film actually begins running backward as evidenced by the smoke moving downward and back into the water pipe. Also, note that the bubbles in his hookah are moving downward.

Oogling at Oola

Oola, one of the slave girls serving in Jabba's court, accidentally "falls out of her costume" during a medium close-up shot when the crime lord tries to drag the dancer toward him. Her breast can be seen for one or two frames of film. (Note: This blooper has been deleted from the VHS letterbox version.)

Another Fashion Statement

When Leia looks out the window on Jabba's sail barge at Han, Luke and Chewie, the Wookiee's bandolier is hanging from his right shoulder to his left hip. In the next shot (when Han says, "3PO, you tell that slimy piece . . ."), notice that Chewie's bandolier is now hanging from his left shoulder to his right hip.

Maybe It Was the Force

During the battle on the skiffs over the Sarlacc pit, Luke swings at Boba Fett with his lightsaber and slices the bounty hunter's weapon in two. If you watch the scene in slow motion, however, you will see that Fett's gun begins to explode one frame before Luke actually destroys it with his saber.

Lando Must Have Learned This Trick From Chewie

When Han and Lando are talking in the Rebel hangar, just before the strike team departs in the stolen Imperial shuttle, *Tydirium*, the gun belt across Lando's chest changes sides between different cuts during the same scene.

C-3PO Is Wired

After R2-D2 rescues his counterpart from Salacious Crumb, C-3PO says, "Well, I can't possibly . . ." and the little droid pushes C-3PO off of the edge of the skiff. Look closely and you will be able to see several wires pulling the droid off of the surface utility vehicle.

The Emperor's Big Steps

After the Emperor lands on the Death Star, he speaks with Darth Vader as they walk slowly past the legions of Imperial troops. At the end of their conversation, there is a tight shot of the Emperor directly in front of a multitude of gray-suited officers. But when the camera cuts to a wide angle shot, the Emperor's background is a seemingly endless mass of white and black clad stormtroopers.

Ambidextrous Luke

During the speeder bike chase on Endor's moon, the glove covering Luke's prosthetic is on his right hand. In the next shot it is on his left, and then back to his right in the third shot before he jumps off and the speeder bike crashes.

Han Must Have Radar

Han attempts to sneak up behind a biker scout but steps on a twig, alerting the Imperial to Solo's presence. The stormtrooper quickly turns and whacks Han in the face. If you pay close attention or slow the videotape to frame-by-frame, you can see that Solo actually begins to recoil from the hit before the trooper even lays a hand on him.

Luke Must Have Been Using the Force . . . Again

Boba Fett is struck by Han and his rocket pack misfires, sending the bounty hunter flying into Tatooine's desert sky. The camera follows Fett's flight for a moment and then cuts to a sceen showing the bow of a skiff. Luke kicks one of Jabba the Hutt's henchmen, but the boy very clearly misses him by a few inches. Nevertheless, the criminal tumbles to his doom in the Sarlacc pit.

Maybe Lando Was Carrying Gloves in His Back Pockets

When Lando is hanging onto the skiff to keep from falling to his death, he is not wearing gloves in any of the close-up shots. Yet, in the wide camera angles, he has black gloves over his hands.

Give Luke a Hand

During the battle on Jabba's sail barge, Luke is on the deck when his hand gets shot, and then it appears scorched and scarred. If you pause the picture for one or two frames before he's hit, you will notice that his hand is already charred. The next time we see Luke's hand is when he is running to get the rope so that he and Leia can swing to safety. During this quick shot, the boy's hand appears to be in perfect condition. But a frame or two later, when he actually retrieves the rope, the audience can attest to the fact that his hand is severely damaged once again. And when the couple swing across the desert, it seems to be magically regenerated. Finally, when Luke departs Tatooine for Dagobah in his starfighter, the hand *really* appears scarred and ravaged by a weapon's blast.

Lando's Vanishing Act

Just before Luke is to be pushed into the Sarlacc pit, he nods at Lando to his *right*. The camera switches to other shots, and when the camera comes back to the skiff guard prodding Luke to take the plunge (and after Jabba orders, "Put him in!"), there is a quick view of Lando, who is now in the background on Luke's *left* side. The succeeding shot shows Luke jumping into the Sarlacc pit with Han and Chewie in the same position Lando was in during the previous camera angle.

Which Way Did They Go?

Moments before the Emperor's shuttle lands aboard the Death Star, a stream of Imperial TIE starfighters are circling the battle station in a parade formation. In the first few frames of this scene, two TIE squadrons fly out from behind the camera toward the main fighter group. Just before the first squadron converges with the principal assemblage, and only a moment or two before the scene concludes, the squadron disappears from the picture.

Han Shows Off His Batman Impersonation

When Luke and Company are about to be thrown into the Sarlacc pit, Han and Lando are standing on the levitating platform. One of Jabba's henchmen fires a shot, effectively hitting the vehicle and causing it to tilt at a precarious angle. As everybody clambers to balance themselves, Han grabs hold of the edge of the ship and desperately hangs on for dear life. A few frames later, however, he is shown hanging by his feet! If you watch closely, though, when Han goes out of view of the camera angle, you can see his shadow as he begins to pull himself up and flip around to hang by his feet.

No Attachments

The swing that Luke and Leia take to get away from Jabba's soon-to-be-destroyed sail barge is physically impossible, as there is nothing to anchor the rope. The angles from their departure, and when the two land, effectively proves that the rope is attached to a point somewhere between the skiff and the sail barge. Unfortunately, on film there is nothing there but the desert of Tatooine.

Course Correction

During Mon Mothma's Rebel briefing on the Empire's second Death Star, the lights darken and a hologram of Endor's moon and the battle station appear in the middle of the conference room. When the hologram begins projecting its three-dimensional images, the Death Star orbits the moon from screen left to screen right. During all subsequent shots of the hologram, the Imperial battle station orbits from right to left.

Try, Try Again

After Leia regains consciousness from her fall off the speeder bike (and encounters Wicket the Ewok), she sits down on a log and takes off her helmet. The camera cuts to another angle that clearly shows it removed, but then a closer shot shows her taking the helmet off again. (Note: This blooper is best viewed on the letterboxed version as you can see the helmet off her head only on the far left of the screen.)

Blondes Have More Fun

During the lightsaber duel between Luke and Darth Vader in the Emperor's throne room aboard the Death Star, there is a scene in which Luke does an Olympic-worthy somersault jump to the floor above. If you look closely at the stunt double's hair, you will notice that it is much more blonde than Mark Hamill's.

Shadow Warriors

During Luke and Vader's climactic battle in the Emperor's throne room, you can see a shadow of the Dark Lord's lightsaber on the battle station floor just after Luke knocks Vader down the stairs and he gets back up on his feet.

Shadow Warriors, Round Two

As Luke and Vader continue to ferociously battle with their lightsabers behind a flight of stairs and then in front of a circular window, the camera cuts to an angle in which the audience looks down upon the duel. The weapons once again cast quite noticeable shadows on the floor of the battle station, especially in the scene just before Luke slices Vader's hand off.

But Can He Pull a Wookiee Out of a Hat

After the Ewoks captured Luke and Company on the moon of Endor, there is a shot of an untied R2-D2, even though at this point in the movie the Ewoks have not yet decided to free the Rebels and help them fight the Imperial forces.

Lando's Insubordination

As the Rebel armada disembarks from their rendezvous at the Sullust star system for their assault on the Death Star battle station, Admiral Ackbar orders, "All craft, prepare to jump into hyperspace on my mark." The camera then cuts to the interior of the *Millennium Falcon,* where Lando says, "Alright. Stand by." Then he abruptly pulls the lever and makes the jump to hyperspace, although Ackbar has still not given the appropriate command.

Han Suffers from Roving Hands Syndrome

After Leia is wounded during the ground battle on Endor's moon, Han grabs her and pulls her back to safety. Pay close attention to his hand—as he fondles her breast!

Endor National Park

After the Rebels have disembarked from the stolen Imperial shuttle, *Tydirium,* the audience can see a redwood fence in the background, of the variety commonly found in U.S. national parks.

Color Scheme

During some scenes, Admiral Piett's blue uniform rank insignia changes color to black, due to the "blue screening" special effect in which everything that is one shade of blue is replaced in post-production with another background.

Two Hans Are Better Than One

As the Imperial bunker on Endor is about to explode from the detonation devices set by the Rebel strike force, Han yells, "Move! Move!" As he distances himself from the building, the second time he calls out "Move!" you can see his reflection behind him, running in the opposite direction. The effect was caused by a sheet of Plexiglas positioned between Harrison Ford and the explosion to protect the actors in case of an accident.

AUTHORS' AFTERWORD:
Back to the Future

"Star Wars was designed as a film for young people. It was done with all the energy, intelligence and thought I could muster."

—George Lucas in a 1981 interview with *Starlog* magazine

"I went in thinking it would be cool, but after the first scene I was screaming. It was the single most important movie in my life."

—Dean Devlin, producer of *Independence Day*, who waited in line for four hours to see *Star Wars* in 1977

A long time ago . . . Well, actually it was twenty years ago at the time of this writing, when George Lucas brought his classic swashbuckling space opera *Star Wars* to movie theaters worldwide. A whole new special-effects factory (Industrial Light & Magic) was constructed to take advantage of computer technology to implement some of the most elaborate miniature and optical effects ever produced for motion pictures. But it was the strength of a simple but powerful story and the heroics of a handful of colorful characters that actually captured our imaginations and transported us to an unknown galaxy thousands of light years from earth.

Looking back, it is hard to believe that in 1977 the eventual critical and commercial bomb *Exorcist II: The Heretic* was expected to be the heavyweight box-office champ of the summer. Even Twentieth Century Fox was telling movie theaters that if they wanted to show Sidney Sheldon's *The Other Side of Midnight,* they would have to book their science-fiction gamble, *Star Wars.*

The film was so ground-breaking and innovative, though, that it changed movie making forever. George Lucas' modern masterpiece was a phenomenon that opened up a new era in special effects by being the first movie to forge a union of cinema and the new video and computer technologies for creating screen images. The last advances in visual technology of that enormity had occurred decades earlier with Willis O'Brien's stop-motion effects for the original *King Kong.* There were visually imaginative films in the transpiring years, notably *Jason and the Argonauts,* Stanley Kubrick's *2001: A Space Odyssey* and *Logan's Run,* but they relied mostly on comprehensive use of models and other pre-existing technologies. But with *Star Wars,* Lucas and his band of gifted young special-effects wizards created movie magic that had never before been seen on the big screen.

Critics, though, shrugged *Star Wars* off as a "kiddie" movie, a live-action version of a Saturday morning cartoon. They saw the story of a young farm boy who gets caught up in the middle of a galactic civil war as overly simplistic, with no characterization, merely eye candy—an updated version of the old Flash Gordon serials. No doubt, those elements certainly exist in *Star Wars,* but the film was the boldest attempt in the modern history of movies to present a true fantasy, a latter-day *Wizard of Oz* in which its characters were on a fateful journey of self-discovery. The audience reaction was nothing short of astounding. Newspapers and television stations across the country reported long lines outside of theaters and snarled traffic jams for the duration of the summer.

After twenty years, how does *Star Wars* hold up to the elements, and to the cinematic blockbusters that it spawned? Oh, sure, the hairstyles are definitely the '70s, some of the special effects have deteriorated over two decades and the final assault on the Death Star is allowed to go on way too long, but if you get caught up in the action and the endearing, but quietly sophisticated story of the movie's humans and aliens, then you will come to realize that *Star Wars* is truly a classically timeless film for the young and the young at heart.

Although entertaining films in their own right, the other two installments in the trilogy did not live up to the standards established by the first movie. Because Lucas obviously placed so much of his creativity into *Star Wars*, for which a whole universe was created, *The Empire Strikes Back* and *Return of the Jedi* simply built upon and amplified that galaxy far, far away. In other words, they took Dad's classic car (which he built from scratch) for a short spin around the block.

In the now legendary Mos Eisley cantina scene, the first film exhibited bizarre-looking, hard-drinking aliens with uncomfortably human characteristics. But in *Return of the Jedi* we got a singing elephant with lips on the end of her nose; Salacious Crumb, an obvious escapee from *The Muppet Show*; slow-witted pig guards; a dancing fat woman; and the worst of the lot, cute and cuddly, teddy bear-like Ewoks. Reportedly, Lucas decided at one point that the third installment would take place in large part on the Wookiee homeworld. But the tall, furry creatures would not have made millions in lovable merchandise and toys, so Lucas reversed the syllables in Wookiee and came up with Ewok. We didn't want any Ewok toys, though. We wanted a stuffed Rancor.

Darth Vader, who was the epitome of evil in the first installment of the trilogy, weakened as a character as the movies progressed. In *Star Wars*, the Dark Lord was presented as being *very* powerful in the dark side of the Force, almost undefeatable. Then in *The Empire Strikes Back*, the audience was introduced to the Galactic Emperor, and suddenly Vader was transformed into a submissive disciple of his dark side "master." Finally, in the trilogy's third installment, *Return of the Jedi*, Vader was nothing more than a lapdog to the Emperor, much the same as Salacious Crumb was to his bloated lord and master, Jabba the Hutt. It was disheartening to witness the loss of character integrity of perhaps the greatest villain to have ever graced movie screens.

Twentieth Century Fox, in a tour de "Force" of marketing savvy, re-released the original trilogy as a boxed set of videocassettes in late 1995 and early 1996, to a whole new global generation (more than nine million units were sold during the first week of the video trilogy's release). And then Lucas took his venerable, revitalized and digitally enhanced classics back to movie theaters in 1997 to commemorate the twentieth anniversary of the first film and to expose the trilogy to the next generation, while reminding the rest of us baby boomers just how special the movie series still is, especially with its $10 million technological face-lift.

With interest in the first trilogy at its highest level since the films were originally released in movie theaters, most conversations among fans revolve around opinions about why the first films were so culturally significant and whether it will be possible for the next trilogy, planned for 1999, to live up to the three original classics.

Lucas has promised that the next three movies will be much more character-driven, more complex in dealing with treachery, and will center largely on Anakin Skywalker before he became Darth Vader. Let's accept the fact that these new movies are *Star Wars* prequels, but let's also view them as independent films in and of themselves rather than having a predetermined attitude of "They can't possibly be as good as the first trilogy."

One thing is certain, though: we'll be there again, standing in line for four hours before the first show.

James Hatfield & George "Doc" Burt

ANSWER KEY

Each correct answer is worth one (1) point. For every Jedi Master Bonus answered correctly, add an additional five (5) points.

STAR POWER, Part One

1. B   2. *Rand Ecliptic*   3. A   4. Kessel   5. A   6. B

Jedi Master Bonus #1: A-wing starfighter

7. False (Four)   8. As greater than half that of the Imperial fleet
9. C   10. C   11. Snowspeeders   12. B

Jedi Master Bonus #2: X-wing fighters, Y-wing fighters, *Millennium Falcon*, Star Destroyers, and TIE fighters

13. A   14. True   15. A   16. B   17. The wings spread apart for attack, forming an X   18. Sail barge

Jedi Master Bonus #3: XP-38

19. C   20. snub   21. C   22. *Executor*   23. A   24. Corvette

Jedi Master Bonus #4: The Headquarters Frigate

25. A planet-destroying superlaser   26. A small thermal exhaust port   27. B   28. "walker"   29. "chicken"   30. B

Jedi Master Bonus #5: 9.2

31. *Slave I*   32. four   33. False (1.6 kilometers)   34. True   35. A T-16 skyhopper   36. A tractor beam

Jedi Master Bonus #6: Sandcrawler, escape pod, landspeeder, Vader's customized TIE fighter, Blockade Runner, and various Mos Eisley spaceport vehicles

37. Round   38. spaceliners   39. Lando Calrissian   40. A   41. It clung to the top of Captain Needa's Star Destroyer, the *Avenger* 42. C

Jedi Master Bonus #7: Snowspeeders and X-wing starfighters

MAXIMUM SCORE POTENTIAL: 77

YOUR SCORE: _____

FROM FARM BOY TO JEDI KNIGHT: Luke Skywalker

1. Owen Lars   2. Ben Kenobi   3. Beru Lars   4. Imperial stormtroopers tracking R2-D2 and C-3PO to the Lars' moisture farm as they searched for the stolen Death Star technical plans stored in R2-D2's memory banks   5. B   6. B

Jedi Master Bonus #1: Fixer

7. C   8. False (Windy)   9. Biggs Darklighter   10. A   11. Old 12. His father's lightsaber

Jedi Master Bonus #2: Uncle Owen needed him on the Tatooine moisture farm for another season

13. C   14. False (right-handed)   15. True   16. From the belt on his stormtrooper uniform   17. His gun   18. Bull's-eyeing womp rats   19. C   20. To take over his training so that the two could rule the Empire together as father and son

Jedi Master Bonus #3: Bacta

21. He used the Force to retrieve his lightsaber and cut himself down from his leg restraints   22. He wanted to investigate a meteorite that crashed nearby   23. Ben Kenobi's spirit form

Jedi Master Bonus #4: Biggs Darklighter

24. True   25. Darth Vader   26. Cloud City and his friends in pain
27. By jumping into an exhaust port

Jedi Master Bonus #5: His hand, his lightsaber, and his innocence (Vader told him Kenobi had lied, that he *was* Luke's father)

Jedi Master Bonus #6: A weather vane

28. B   29. A   30. A vivid green   31. R2-D2   32. True

Jedi Master Bonus #7: Voice Manipulation

33. friend   34. C   35. Ben Kenobi's spirit form   36. Luke (albeit unintentionally, when his thoughts betrayed him)

Jedi Master Bonus #8: feeble

Jedi Master Bonus #9: Eighteen

MAXIMUM SCORE POTENTIAL: 81

YOUR SCORE: _____

I, Robot

1. C   2. Astromech   3. They'd be sent to the Kessel spice mines or "smashed into who-knows-what"   4. Probe droids   5. B   6. B

Jedi Master Bonus #1: To the south ridge to work on the condensers

7. True   8. A   9. Talkdroid   10. C   11. Six   12. A

Jedi Master Bonus #2: Phlutdroid

13. The escape pod registered no life-forms   14. True   15. metal
16. C   17. To have the droid's memory erased   18. True

Jedi Master Bonus #3: 1) to repair a small hit 2) lock down a stabilizer that broke loose and 3) increase the spacecraft's power

19. B   20. False (binary load lifters)   21. carbon   22. philosopher
23. A   24. B

Jedi Master Bonus #4: Repulsorlift

25. False (droids served as human-droid relations specialists)
26. A   27. C   28. False (Female voice)   29. voice   30. six   31. A

Jedi Master Bonus #5: Visual, auditory, olfactory and sensory

32. C   33. Restraining bolt   34. Remotes   35. protocol   36. Re-activate switch   37. Memory flush

Jedi Master Bonus #6: Locomotor

38. Photoreceptors   39. Power droids   40. traps   41. Motivator
42. True   43. The technical readouts from the Death Star

Jedi Master Bonus #7: R2 units

44. False (Fourth degree)   45. C   46. Programming binary load lifters   47. A   48. Probot (or probe droid)   49. Circuits or gears

Jedi Master Bonus #8: 3720:1

50. B   51. C   52. True   53. B   54. Blue   55. juicing   56. One

Jedi Master Bonus #9: 1.05

57. C   58. Through a vacuum tube   59. A destroyed sandcrawler
60. True   61. True   62. He put the droid's head on backward
63. True

Jedi Master Bonus #10: Thermocapsulary dehousing assister

Jedi Master Bonus #11: Zone 12, moving east

MAXIMUM SCORE POTENTIAL: 118

YOUR SCORE: _____

BEHIND-THE-SCENES: Star Wars: A New Hope

1. A   2. False (scuba regulator)   3. Mirrors, which reflected the terrain   4. Reel 2, Dialog 2   5. C   6. True

Jedi Master Bonus #1: 60 feet long & 16 feet high

7. B   8. A   9. Vista Vision   10. C   11. C   12. True

Jedi Master Bonus #2: The escape pod leaving Princess Leia's Rebel Blockade Runner

13. Director's Guild of America (DGA)   14. Lucas' dog, Indiana (Care to guess the origin of Indiana Jones' name?)   15. True   16. B   17. False (Harrison Ford)   18. A

Jedi Master Bonus #3: A pedestrian leading a Ronto, a large beast of burden, on a leash

19. C   20. True   21. C   22. 20th Century Records   23. B   24. B

Jedi Master Bonus #4: Grant McCune

25. He believed it had the greatest chance of being a commercial success   26. True   27. A   28. Jabba the Hutt. In any reference prior to 1983, the "official" spelling included only one "T"   29. B

Jedi Master Bonus #5: Other traffic in the skies over the spaceport

30. A   31. False (March 1976)   32. Tunisia's native architecture was closer to what Lucas had in mind for the desert of Tatooine   33. C   34. Tomlinson Holman's eXperiment. Holman, the inventor of the THX sound system, is a good friend of George Lucas   35. B

Jedi Master Bonus #6: Yuma, Arizona

36. C   37. Steven Spielberg   38. B   39. True   40. A   41. B

Jedi Master Bonus #7: $2 million

42. False (twenty-four)   43. Alec Guinness and Peter Cushing   44. True   45. Four   46. C   47. seven

Jedi Master Bonus #8: 1, 5, 3, 2, 4

48. B   49. Chewie   50. C   51. David Prowse   52. True   53. C
54. B   55. False (from production artist Ralph McQuarrie's illustrations)   56. Scotchlite   57. True

Jedi Master Bonus #9: 95

Jedi Master Bonus #10: A stormtrooper, his trusty dewback, the dewback's looming shadow, the creature's footprints in the sand, and an Imperial transport in the sky

Jedi Master Bonus #11: *The Special Edition*'s **dewbacks were more lizardlike, with smaller, more birdlike legs. They also moved at a very sluggish and uncomfortable pace**

58. C   59. A   60. C-3PO's Anthony Daniels   61. True   62. The Mos Eisley cantina scene   63. PepsiCo   64. True

Jedi Master Bonus #12: $5 million

65. At the time, there was no way to make Jabba "mobile"   66. Boba Fett   67. *Carrie*   68. B   69. Stan Winston   70. True   71. True

Jedi Master Bonus #13: Koo Stark

72. nine   73. B   74. A scene in which her character was hung upside down and tortured   75. Vader is the Dutch word for "father," and his intention with the name Darth Vader was to evoke "dark father"   76. True   77. C   78. B   79. *THX-1138*

Jedi Master Bonus #14: The name simply "popped" into his head one day

Jedi Master Bonus #15: *Independence Day*

MAXIMUM SCORE POTENTIAL: 154
YOUR SCORE: _____

THE NAME GAME: Star Wars: A New Hope

1. E   2. H   3. B   4. G   5. K   6. C   7. L   8. D   9. A   10. F
11. J   12. I

MAXIMUM SCORE POTENTIAL: 12

YOUR SCORE: _____

Star Tech

1. Transfer registers   2. damper   3. Hyperdrive   4. Gameboard
5. Pressors   6. Shield

Jedi Master Bonus #1: Seven

7. Main drive   8. B   9. Comlinks   10. C   11. True   12. A

Jedi Master Bonus #2: .5 past light speed

13. Macrofuser   14. Light table   15. ion   16. True   17. Central
lifter   18. Nine

Jedi Master Bonus #3: Fusioncutter and hydrospanner

19. Repulsorlift engine   20. claws   21. B   22. paralight   23. Reversion   24. Seeker   25. He cut the sublight engines   26. C

Jedi Master Bonus #4: 3 times: fleeing Hoth, leaving the asteroid belt, and in their exodus from Cloud City

Jedi Master Bonus #5: The horizontal boosters and alluvial dampers

27. Approach vector   28. Breath mask   29. Cloaking device
30. A   31. B   32. Light speed

Jedi Master Bonus #6: 1) it captured ships 2) dumped garbage and 3) deployed probots

33. Lift tube   34. True   35. particle   36. Power converter
37. Power coupling   38. C   39. A   40. Antigrav drive

Jedi Master Bonus #7: Condenser unit

41. B   42. Electro-jabber   43. towers   44. Electrotelescope
45. False (Freeze-floating control)   46. C

Jedi Master Bonus #8: 3263827

47. Fusion furnaces   48. Servodriver   49. C   50. True   51. Phototropic shielding   52. A   53. False (hydrospanner)   54. Horizontal booster   55. True

Jedi Master Bonus #9: Fusioncutter

56. A   57. A   58. Macrobinoculars   59. B   60. A long, thin repulsorlift unipod

Jedi Master Bonus #10: Hyperdrive motivator

MAXIMUM SCORE POTENTIAL: 110

YOUR SCORE: _____

ALIEN FACES & PLACES, Part I

1. Ugnaught   2. True   3. Jawas   4. C   5. Dianoga   6. A

Jedi Master Bonus #1: Tosche Station

7. False (Tatoo 1, Tatoo II)   8. Wampa ice creature   9. Mos Eisley   10. C   11. Max Rebo   12. B

Jedi Master Bonus #2: Kessel

13. False (indigenous to Alderaan)   14. True   15. Nikto   16. slug   17. Sy Snootles   18. A

Jedi Master Bonus #3: Remains of a Rebel base

19. A   20. Hoth   21. Jawas   22. Alderaan   23. Banthas   24. B

Jedi Master Bonus #4: Bothan

25. C   26. Kitonak   27. Great Pit of Carkoon   28. B   29. False (Heater)   30. Pote Snitkin

Jedi Master Bonus #5: Dark blue with gold trim

31. A   32. B   33. True   34. Tusken Raiders   35. A   36. C

Jedi Master Bonus #6: Derra IV

37. B   38. A   39. Captain Antilles   40. Bubo   41. A   42. True

Jedi Master Bonus #7: White

43. Krayt dragons   44. B   45. Mon Calamari   46. B   47. Night-crawlers   48. Oola

Jedi Master Bonus #8: Outer Rim Territories

49. They burned them   50. No one asked to see their identification or landing permit   51. C   52. bad

MAXIMUM SCORE POTENTIAL: 92

YOUR SCORE: _____

THE WAN AND OBI: Ben Kenobi

1. General   2. Yoda   3. Bail Organa and Anakin Skywalker   4. Anakin Skywalker   5. He hid Skywalker's children from him, and then Kenobi went into hiding   6. western

Jedi Master Bonus #1: He gave a krayt dragon call

7. Luke's Uncle Owen   8. The Bantha tracks were side-by-side instead of single file, and the blaster marks were too accurate   9. A helmet with its blast shield down   10. C   11. B   12. His cloak and lightsaber   13. Tapped it with his boot

Jedi Master Bonus #2: "Run, Luke, run"

14. A   15. seduced   16. His feelings   17. destiny

Jedi Master Bonus #3: "My little friend"

Jedi Master Bonus #4: surrounds

MAXIMUM SCORE POTENTIAL: 37

YOUR SCORE: _____

Ewok This Way

1. B   2. A   3. All Terrain Scout Transport (AT-ST) or better known as "chicken" and "scout walker"   4. C   5. Hang gliders
6. True

Jedi Master Bonus #1: Paploo

7. False (Wiley and Nippett)   8. B   9. A   10. The half skull of a great forest bird   11. C   12. Wicket W. Warrick

Jedi Master Bonus #2: One

13. True   14. C   15. A horned half skull decorated with feathers
16. Wicket W. Warrick   17. Wicket W. Warrick   18. Luke Skywalker

Jedi Master Bonus #3: Chief Chirpa

19. C-3PO   20. B   21. C-3PO   22. Chief Chirpa

MAXIMUM SCORE POTENTIAL: 37

YOUR SCORE: _____

REBEL RUMBLINGS & IMPERIAL TRANSMISSIONS
Star Wars: A New Hope

1. B   2. Dantooine   3. reactor   4. B   5. C   6. False (C-3PO made the comment)

Jedi Master Bonus #1: Ben Kenobi

7. restricted   8. C-3PO   9. C   10. Han Solo   11. consciously
12. thousand

Jedi Master Bonus #2: Ben Kenobi

13. circle   14. revolution   15. A   16. Darth Vader   17. C   18. B

Jedi Master Bonus #3: Han Solo

19. harvest   20. Beru Owens   21. C-3PO   22. modifications
23. Grand Moff Tarkin   24. B

Jedi Master Bonus #4: twenty

25. Han Solo   26. True   27. Grand Moff Tarkin   28. larger
29. decoy   30. A   31. straight   32. C-3PO   33. C-3PO   34. destiny   35. Princess Leia to a disguised Luke   36. tremor

Jedi Master Bonus #5: fire

Jedi Master Bonus #6: Vader (by Tarkin)

37. B   38. Luke, when the *Millennium Falcon* approached the Death Star and Han, when the walls of the trash compactor started to move in   39. Leia   40. Ben Kenobi   41. Han Solo   42. commission

Jedi Master Bonus #7: Princess Leia

43. Grand Moff Tarkin   44. mercenary   45. Princess Leia
46. logic   47. Darth Vader   48. B

Jedi Master Bonus #8: served, struggle, mission, struggle, desperate

49. C   50. damage   51. C-3PO   52. Biggs, Tank   53. terror
54. True

Jedi Master Bonus #9: sorcerer's, clairvoyance

55. A   56. B   57. joints   58. Grand Moff Tarkin   59. Darth Vader
60. Darth Vader

Jedi Master Bonus #10: Jabba the Hutt

61. supernova   62. terror   63. False (C-3PO admitted that he was "not very good at telling stories")   64. General Tagge   65. conscious   66. C   67. B   68. True

Jedi Master Bonus #11: Biggs Darklighter

MAXIMUM SCORE POTENTIAL: 123

YOUR SCORE: _____

Star Warfare

1. B   2. True   3. Targeting computer   4. thermal   5. Two   6. Four

Jedi Master Bonus #1: Two quad laser cannons and two concussion missile launchers

7. Two   8. C   9. Bowcaster   10. A   11. B   12. two, two

Jedi Master Bonus #2: In a concealed compartment in the freighter's lower hull

13. B   14. Ion cannon   15. retractable   16. C   17. True   18. A

Jedi Master Bonus #3: Blaster

19. True   20. laser   21. A   22. Concussion missiles   23. energy   24. C

Jedi Master Bonus #4: Twenty-nine

25. A   26. In the top and bottom turrets   27. B   28. False   29. quarrels   30. True   31. harpoon

Jedi Master Bonus #5: five

32. True   33. Round   34. C   35. A   36. cryogenic   37. True

Jedi Master Bonus #6: Energy call

38. mini-ion   39. Gaffi stick   40. False (spherical towers)   41. True   42. True   43. twin

Jedi Master Bonus #7: 15,000

MAXIMUM SCORE POTENTIAL: 78

YOUR SCORE: _____

PRINCESS BY VIRTUE, REBEL BY CHOICE: Leia Organa

1. Bail Organa   2. B   3. The Clone Wars   4. C   5. True   6. A

Jedi Master Bonus #1: Cell 2187

7. Her capture might have generated sympathy for the Rebellion in the Imperial Senate   8. He ordered a distress signal emitted from the *Tantive IV* and then reported that all aboard were killed   9. B   10. Diplomatic   11. A   12. Dantooine

Jedi Master Bonus #2: Four

Jedi Master Bonus #3: Chalcedony waves

13. Via a hologram   14. B   15. White   16. False (a Wookiee)

Jedi Master Bonus #4: Leia, Your Highness, Sweetheart, Your Worship, Your Worshipfulness, Sister, Your Highness, and Princess

17. She was forced to be one of Jabba's slave girls   18. B   19. Beneath the swaying trees of the Ewok village on Endor

Jedi Master Bonus #5: Block AA-23

MAXIMUM SCORE POTENTIAL: 44

YOUR SCORE: _____

SMUGGLER'S BLUES: Han Solo

1. Corellia   2. A   3. C

Jedi Master Bonus #1: 17,000; two in advance and fifteen when Han reached Alderaan

4. "Sorry about the mess"   5. C   6. force, mystical   7. He fired his blaster, which ricocheted   8. Luke   9. Han told Luke he wasn't going to let him get all the credit and take all the reward   10. A death mark, a bounty for his capture—dead or alive!   11. Luke's lightsaber

Jedi Master Bonus #2: The Rebel mechanics were having trouble adapting the snowspeeders [airspeeders] to the cold

12. Lando Calrissian   13. Boba Fett   14. Carbonite

Jedi Master Bonus #3: Hibernation sickness

15. Chewie

Jedi Master Bonus #4: Mon Mothma and her Advisory Council

MAXIMUM SCORE POTENTIAL: 35

YOUR SCORE: _____

WANTED: Dead or Alive

1. B   2. C   3. Greedo   4. B   5. S-thread   6. A

Jedi Master Bonus #1: Metallic

7. 4-LOM   8. C   9. True   10. Mandalore   11. C   12. False (Beedo was Greedo's relative)

Jedi Master Bonus #2: Two

13. macrobinocular   14. Wookiee scalps   15. A   16. B   17. True
18. comlink   19. turbo   20. True

Jedi Master Bonus #3: 100, 70

Jedi Master Bonus #4: Ord Mantrell

MAXIMUM SCORE POTENTIAL: 40

YOUR SCORE: _____

SOLO'S SIDEKICK: Chewbacca

1. B   2. Either his massive fists or his bowcaster   3. Mechanic
4. two   5. True

Jedi Master Bonus #1: Two

6. Princess Leia   7. Severely damaged droids

Jedi Master Bonus #2: "Save your strength. . . . There'll be another time."

8. He persuaded Han to go back and assist his Rebel friends, which gave Luke enough time to effectively destroy the original Death Star battle station   9. He helped rally the Ewoks into a fighting force, which allowed the Rebel strike team time to sabotage the shield generator protecting the second Death Star 10. Grunts, growls and roars   11. "Alien prisoner"   12. Lando Calrissian

Jedi Master Bonus #3: He reached out and grabbed dead animal meat which was used as a bait on a stake that sprung the suspension net's operating mechanism

MAXIMUM SCORE POTENTIAL: 27

YOUR SCORE: _____

BEHIND-THE-SCENES: The Empire Strikes Back

1. C   2. False (A little more than 100)   3. B   4. A potato 5. True   6. A

Jedi Master Bonus #1: King snakes and boa constrictors

7. B   8. Leigh Brackett and Lawrence Kasdan   9. True   10. B 11. C   12. True

Jedi Master Bonus #2: The end of a lamp post from the street outside the ILM building

13. The scene in which Luke received facial scars from a Wampa ice creature   14. Irvin Kershner   15. False (May 21, 1980) 16. His material dream, Skywalker Ranch   17. In California 18. True   19. B   20. True

Jedi Master Bonus #3: C-3PO

21. C   22. five   23. A   24. C   25. True   26. B   27. Brian Daley
28. David Prowse   29. True   30. B

Jedi Master Bonus #4: *People*

Jedi Master Bonus #5: Five

31. True   32. Oakland   33. True   34. Billy Dee Williams   35. B
36. B   37. Gary Kurtz   38. A

Jedi Master Bonus #6: Sound, Special Achievement Award for Visual Effects

Jedi Master Bonus #7: 18 sessions of three hours each spread over a period of two weeks

Jedi Master Bonus #8: 117

39. thirty   40. True   41. It was the "middle act of a three-act play" , 42. A   43. Jim Hensen (who recommended Frank Oz)
44. C   45. False   46. True

Jedi Master Bonus #9: The Cloud City scenes

47. B   48. Elstree Studios   49. A   50. B   51. False (*Empire* required 400 to 500 optical composites)   52. True

Jedi Master Bonus #10: platter

53. C   54. B   55. The *Executor*   56. Chi

Jedi Master Bonus #11: Creature maker/stop motion animator Phil Tippett

Jedi Master Bonus #12: Richard Edlund

Jedi Master Bonus #13: Blue

Jedi Master Bonus #14: Stuart Freeborn

Jedi Master Bonus #15: Jon Berg and Tom St. Amand

Jedi Master Bonus #16: Finse

MAXIMUM SCORE POTENTIAL: 136

YOUR SCORE: _____

THE NAME GAME: The Empire Strikes Back

1. E   2. H   3. K   4. D   5. J   6. A   7. I   8. C   9. L   10. F
11. G   12. B

Jedi Master Bonus #1: Clive Revill

Jedi Master Bonus #2: Jack Purvis

Jedi Master Bonus #3: Kathryn Mullen

Jedi Master Bonus #4: Coburn Howard

MAXIMUM SCORE POTENTIAL: 32

YOUR SCORE: _____

Rebels with a Cause

1. Biggs Darklighter   2. B   3. A   4. Dak   5. Dutch   6. C

Jedi Master Bonus #1: Echo Station Three-Eight

7. Mon Mothma   8. B   9. C   10. True   11. Several transmissions were beamed to the ship by Rebel spies   12. Ackbar

Jedi Master Bonus #2: Pops

13. C   14. False (Red Two)   15. A   16. True   17. C

Jedi Master Bonus #3: K-one-zero

Jedi Master Bonus #4: Skyhook

18. A   19. C   20. Yavin   21. Red Four   22. B   23. Boss
24. Luke Skywalker   25. Madine

Jedi Master Bonus #5: Han Solo

26. B   27. False (Battle of Endor)   28. four   29. A   30. Wedge Antilles   31. B

Jedi Master Bonus #6: General Dodonna

32. True   33. A-wing   34. Echo Base   35. C   36. True   37. True
38. Hobbie

Jedi Master Bonus #7: Janson

39. A harpoon with a tow cable attached to it   40. Rebellion
41. Crix   42. A   43. C   44. C   45. Orange (with some white and gray)

Jedi Master Bonus #8: Wedge Antilles

MAXIMUM SCORE POTENTIAL: 85

YOUR SCORE: _____

ALIEN FACES & PLACES, Part II

1. False (Barada)   2. C   3. The fourth moon   4. B   5. C
6. Toprawa

Jedi Master Bonus #1: Gundark

7. True   8. Beggar's Canyon   9. Bespin   10. A   11. False (the Dagobah Star System)   12. Bib Fortuna

Jedi Master Bonus #2: Fornax

13. B   14. True   15. A   16. True   17. False (Ishi Tib was bipedal with a birdlike beak)   18. B

Jedi Master Bonus #3: "No blasters. No blasters."

19. nerfs   20. C   21. Salacious Crumb   22. sandwhirls   23. B
24. C

Jedi Master Bonus #4: He had an elephant's trunk for a nose

25. Tauntauns 26. Anchorhead 27. Dune 28. A 29. True 30. False (five meters)

Jedi Master Bonus #5: Gray

31. B 32. Tatooine 33. C 34. Three 35. Four 36. They were massacred by Imperial stormtroopers

Jedi Master Bonus #6: 1000

37. Gray or gray spotted 38. Males 39. B 40. True 41. True 42. C

Jedi Master Bonus #7: Mynocks

43. *Star Wars* 44. False (tech domes) 45. False (Tatooine) 46. B

Jedi Master Bonus #8: The Anoat System

47. A 48. Droids 49. B

Jedi Master Bonus #9: Twi'lek

Jedi Master Bonus #10: Sluis

MAXIMUM SCORE POTENTIAL: 99

YOUR SCORE: _____

LORD OF THE DARK SIDE: Darth Vader

1. The Clone Wars 2. Obi-Wan Kenobi 3. idealistic 4. Obi-Wan Kenobi 5. During a fight with Obi-Wan he fell into a molten pit 6. Hunt down and exterminate Jedi Knights

Jedi Master Bonus #1: The Sith

7. He thought the Rebellion would be destroyed 8. A 9. Clipped to his belt 10. Darth Vader, Lord of the Sith 11. Lord Vader 12. The fleet assigned to track down Luke Sky-walker

Jedi Master Bonus #2: Aboard the *Super*-class Star Destroyer *Executor*

13. He told Lando Calrissian they must never leave Cloud City, and then decided to take them aboard his ship as prisoners
14. He used the dark side of the Force to hurl objects at his son
15. To rule the galaxy as father and son

Jedi Master Bonus #3: ST 321

Jedi Master Bonus #4: "You were right about me. Tell your sister . . . you were right."

MAXIMUM SCORE POTENTIAL: 35

YOUR SCORE: _____

REBEL RUMBLINGS & IMPERIAL TRANSMISSIONS: The Empire Strikes Back

1. motion   2. fear   3. General Rieekan   4. B   5. False (sixth planet)   6. The Emperor

Jedi Master Bonus #1: "No . . . no . . . no. Quicker, easier, more seductive."

7. B   8. C   9. B   10. swindler   11. Obi-Wan Kenobi   12. conquer
13. Yoda   14. False (Leia made the comment as she dabbed at his wounds)

Jedi Master Bonus #2: prize

15. Darth Vader   16. B   17. C   18. conflict   19. The destruction of the Emperor   20. R2-D2

Jedi Master Bonus #3: "Luke . . . it is your destiny."

21. Han Solo   22. A   23. Admiral Ozzel   24. Dak   25. B
26. False (Leia called the freighter a "bucket of bolts")   27. A
28. scoundrel

Jedi Master Bonus #4: Slimy mudhole

29. True   30. A   31. B   32. Princess Leia   33. C   34. knowledge

Jedi Master Bonus #5: "A domain of evil"

35. methods   36. B   37. True   38. Lando Calrissian   39. Lando Calrissian   40. C   41. "Luke, don't give in to hate—that leads to the dark side."

Jedi Master Bonus #6: socket

Jedi Master Bonus #7: C-3PO

Jedi Master Bonus #8: R2-D2 (by C-3PO)

42. mushy   43. A   44. thermal   45. B   46. B   47. C-3PO   48. gorgeous   49. True   50. C   51. B

Jedi Master Bonus #9: Admiral Ozzel (according to Darth Vader)

Jedi Master Bonus #10: Hobbie

Jedi Master Bonus #11: Princess Leia

52. B   53. tow   54. General Veers   55. General Veers   56. Princess Leia   57. A   58. Han Solo   59. Han Solo

Jedi Master Bonus #12: "Never tell me the odds."

60. C   61. technology

Jedi Master Bonus #13: "Is it safe for droids?"

62. B   63. Luke Skywalker   64. C   65. A   66. held   67. Yoda (to Luke Skywalker)   68. A   69. dialect   70. "Your Worship"   71. B

Jedi Master Bonus #14: reverse

72. Captain Needa   73. C   74. Darth Vader   75. A   76. False ("the deepest commitment, the most serious mind")   77. A   78. B

Jedi Master Bonus #15: "Anger . . . fear . . . aggression"

Jedi Master Bonus #16: dominate

Jedi Master Bonus #17: "Only what you take with you"

79. Princess Leia   80. Captain Needa   81. Luke never believed
82. C-3PO   83. C   84. Being responsible   85. "To return and finish" his Jedi training   86. Obi-Wan Kenobi   87. learned
88. Boba Fett   89. Han Solo   90. Darth Vader

Jedi Master Bonus #18: Princess Leia

Jedi Master Bonus #19: C-3PO

MAXIMUM SCORE POTENTIAL: 185

YOUR SCORE: _____

APPEARANCES CAN BE DECEIVING: Jedi Master Yoda

1. eight   2. Dagobah   3. Nine hundred years old   4. B

Jedi Master Bonus #1: Rootleaf

5. Wars   6. A tiny power lamp   7. "How you get so big, eating
food of this kind?"   8. "Rest . . . forever sleep."   9. Two rocks the
size of bowling balls

Jedi Master Bonus #2: "Size matters not."

10. The power of the Emperor   11. Yoda's species was never
identified   12. Confronting his father, Darth Vader

MAXIMUM SCORE POTENTIAL: 22

YOUR SCORE: _____

The Evil Empire

1. Grand Moff   2. C   3. B   4. General Veers   5. He brought the
task force out of hyperspace within Hoth's sensor range   6. A

Jedi Master Bonus #1: Standard Time Part

7. Admiral Motti   8. Imperial Royal Guard   9. B   10. Grand Moff Tarkin   11. A   12. Tarkin

Jedi Master Bonus #2: Piett, Ozzel, Veers and Needa

13. He refused to evacuate the Death Star prior to its destruction by Rebel forces   14. B   15. False (Five Star Destroyers)   16. Captain Needa   17. The Emperor   18. *Avenger*

Jedi Master Bonus #3: Cass

19. The Emperor   20. The out-of-the-way system had few planets, and no major spaceports or travel routes, an ideal location for a covert and top-secret construction site   21. C   22. Grand Moff Tarkin   23. C   24. A

Jedi Master Bonus #4: Lieutenant Hija

25. False (Sate Pestage)   26. B   27. Black   28. B   29. Governor Tarkin, Admiral Motti and General Tagge   30. Grand Moff Tarkin

Jedi Master Bonus #5: Eighteen

Jedi Master Bonus #6: Jhoff

MAXIMUM SCORE POTENTIAL: 60

YOUR SCORE: _____

MASTER OF THE DARK SIDE: Emperor Palpatine
(NOTE: Each correct answer will count as a 5-point JEDI MASTER BONUS)

Jedi Master Bonus #1: President

Jedi Master Bonus #2: Mon Mothma

Jedi Master Bonus #3: Members of the Senate who once served with him

Jedi Master Bonus #4: emergency

Jedi Master Bonus #5: remnants

Jedi Master Bonus #6: Emperor's Throne Room

Jedi Master Bonus #7: "Yes, I know."

Jedi Master Bonus #8: "aggressive"

Jedi Master Bonus #9: "Now, young Skywalker . . . you will die."

MAXIMUM SCORE POTENTIAL: 45

YOUR SCORE: _____

GAMBLER'S LUCK: The Lowdown on Lando Calrissian

1. B   2. Courtesy of a winning hand of sabacc   3. A deal to keep the Empire out of the Bespin system forever if he would betray Han Solo   4. B   5. Lobot

Jedi Master Bonus #1: Code-Force-Seven

6. Han punched Lando   7. Han Solo   8. supply   9. He was frightened that the Empire would find out about the small gas-producing plant and "shut it down"   10. "Alive . . . and in perfect hibernation"   11. Chewie   12. General

Jedi Master Bonus #2: Norulac

13. He led the Rebel starfighter assault on the second Death Star
14. Nien Numb   15. Wedge Antilles

Jedi Master Bonus #3: Concussion missiles

MAXIMUM SCORE POTENTIAL: 30

YOUR SCORE: _____

BEHIND-THE-SCENES: Return of the Jedi

1. B   2. B   3. Lando Calrissian   4. False (Greek)   5. C   6. So that pirated merchandise could be easily spotted when the film was released

Jedi Master Bonus #1: Body by David Prowse, voice by James Earl Jones, and face by Sebastion Shaw

7. B   8. A birthmark   9. A   10. C   11. Special Achievement Award for Visual Effects   12. C   13. C

Jedi Master Bonus #2: They were named after the command phrase given to the robot Gort in the sci-fi classic *The Day the Earth Stood Still*

14. A   15. B   16. The soft green spotlight used to accentuate the Emperor's eyes spilt over onto objects that should not have been lit. The optics crew then manually blacked out the "overflowing" areas   17. It is a scrambled version of "three-eyes," which the alien had   18. B   19. B

Jedi Master Bonus #3: After Jabba's sail barge was blown up, Luke, Han, Leia and Company had to fight their way through a sandstorm to make it back to their ships

20. six   21. True   22. cereal   23. C   24. A   25. A   26. True   27. George Lucas

Jedi Master Bonus #4: Joe Johnston

28. B   29. B

Jedi Master Bonus #5: George Lucas, director Richard Marquand, Lawrence Kasdan, and producer Howard Kazanjian

30. *Rolling Stone* magazine   31. A   32. The Death Star's main docking bay   33. Three (two men under the floor and one on the catwalk)   34. True   35. True   36. A   37. Anthony Daniels

Jedi Master Bonus #6: Forty-five

38. 35,000 dune buggy enthusiasts   39. C   40. C   41. True
42. Seventy-two   43. B

Jedi Master Bonus #7: *The Empire Strikes Back's* director, Irvin Kershner

44. True   45. A   46. C   47. The midgets looked like men in suits, but the dwarves weren't so symmetrically built, which made them more believable as alien life-forms   48. They were too hard, and the actors couldn't feel the terrain they were walking on, which was dangerous considering one of the sets was 30 feet off the ground   49. B   50. A   51. False (five months to construct)
52. True   53. Anthony Daniels   54. True   55. B

Jedi Master Bonus #8: Mark Hamill

56. True   57. False *(Classic Creatures: Return of the Jedi)*   58. A
59. *The Ewoks/Droids Adventure Hour.* It was renewed for a second season in 1986, but Lucasfilms opted to go with a half-hour show that only featured the Ewoks   60. True   61. Steven Spielberg
62. U.S. and England   63. B   64. Dwarves don't walk or climb ladders as easily as midgets, so they required more "practice runs"
65. C

Jedi Master Bonus #9: *The Ewok Adventure: Caravan of Courage* and *The Ewoks: Battle for Endor*

Jedi Master Bonus #10: Elton John

Jedi Master Bonus #11: Bespin, Tatooine, and Coruscant

66. Sydney Greenstreet   67. ten   68. B   69. Harrison Ford, but Lucas disagreed   70. C   71. A   72. False ($1 million)

Jedi Master Bonus #12: Two hundred

73. True   74. A foam latex hand puppet   75. A   76. four
77. True   78. Phil Tippett, the film's creature design supervisor
79. Nien Nunb   80. C

Jedi Master Bonus #13: "Horror Beyond Imagination"

Jedi Master Bonus #14: eight

Jedi Master Bonus #15: John Lithgow (Yoda), Brock Peters (Darth Vader), Ed Begley (Boba Fett), Perry King (Han Solo), Ann Sachs (Princess Leia), & Ed Asner (Jabba the Hutt)

Jedi Master Bonus #16: Chris Evans

Jedi Master Bonus #17: three

MAXIMUM SCORE POTENTIAL: 165

YOUR SCORE: _____

THE NAME GAME: Return of the Jedi

1. I   2. F   3. H   4. E   5. C   6. K   7. B   8. G   9. J   10. A
11. D   12. L

Jedi Master Bonus #1: Claire Davenport

Jedi Master Bonus #2: Toby Philpott, Mike Edmonds, and David Barclay

Jedi Master Bonus #3: Nick Morrison

Jedi Master Bonus #4: Pip Miller and Tom Mannion

MAXIMUM SCORE POTENTIAL: 32

YOUR SCORE: _____

STAR POWER, Part II

1. True   2. Sail barge   3. The log stated that the crew had abandoned ship, and the escape pod had jettisoned   4. True   5. C
6. B

Jedi Master Bonus #1: two

7. True   8. A   9. B   10. million   11. A   12. Two

Jedi Master Bonus #2: All Terrain Armored Transport and All Terrain Scout Transport

13. C   14. True   15. suspension   16. False   17. B-wing   18. C

Jedi Master Bonus #3: 12.5 meters

19. Two   20. One   21. A   22. B   23. False (These vessels carried little or no armament)   24. True

Jedi Master Bonus #4: Two

25. True   26. B   27. A   28. Ship garbage and sections of irreparable machinery   29. C   30. To destroy the Rebel's power generator

Jedi Master Bonus #5: Five

31. True   32. R2-D2 plugged into a computer outlet   33. *Victory*   34. At the forward end of the saddle seat   35. False (approximately twenty-seven meters)   36. True

Jedi Master Bonus #6: Corellians

37. Medical frigate   38. B   39. False (through a lower hatch)   40. broadband   41. True   42. True   43. thirty

Jedi Master Bonus #7: 120

Jedi Master Bonus #8: 21.5, *Firespray*

Jedi Master Bonus #9: 8,000

MAXIMUM SCORE POTENTIAL: 88

YOUR SCORE: _____

REBEL RUMBLINGS & IMPERIAL TRANSMISSIONS: Return of the Jedi

1. C   2. A carbonized Han Solo   3. Bounty hunter Boushh
4. Bantha   5. C   6. R2-D2

Jedi Master Bonus #1: reckless

7. nature   8. A   9. C   10. B   11. True   12. Salacious Crumb
13. Vader's revelation to Luke that he was his father

Jedi Master Bonus #2: "There is . . . another . . . Sky . . . Sky . . . walker."

Jedi Master Bonus #3: 47

14. C   15. deity   16. A   17. short   18. Han   19. B   20. Vader

Jedi Master Bonus #4: band, legion

21. C   22. B   23. A   24. EV-9D9   25. EV-9D9   26. Ubese

Jedi Master Bonus #5: "Bo Shuda!"

27. True   28. "Rest" and eternal "sleep"   29. Twilight   30. C
31. Han   32. C   33. A   34. The Imperial shuttle *Tydirium*

Jedi Master Bonus #6: R2-D2

Jedi Master Bonus #7: feelings

35. sensors   36. Chewie   37. divine   38. B   39. False (Luke made the demand of C-3PO)   40. Leia

Jedi Master Bonus #8: His "hate"

Jedi Master Bonus #9: Blue

41. B   42. Moff Jerjerrod   43. C   44. Jabba the Hutt   45. A

Jedi Master Bonus #10: "Zeebuss"

46. "Someone who loves you"   47. triple   48. A   49. Han Solo
50. Bib Fortuna   51. False (C-3PO translated Jabba's death sentence)

Jedi Master Bonus #11: "You will take me to Jabba now!"

52. Han Solo   53. search   54. True   55. C   56. The truth about
Anakin Skywalker's "death" by Darth Vader   57. cling   58. consequences

Jedi Master Bonus #12: perimeter

59. B   60. A   61. Han (speaking of the *Millennium Falcon*)
62. Sullust   63. The Sarlacc creature   64. The gangster's refusal
to bargain   65. A

Jedi Master Bonus #13: honorably

Jedi Master Bonus #14: "Oh . . . great!"

66. False (Luke issued the warning)   67. True   68. training
69. Obi-Wan Kenobi   70. C   71. Luke's first encounter with
Vader   72. His feelings   73. Lando Calrissian

Jedi Master Bonus #15: lineage, title

Jedi Master Bonus #16: vain

74. The Emperor   75. B   76. His compassion for his father
77. C-3PO   78. Using his "divine influence" to arrange their release from the Ewoks

Jedi Master Bonus #17: "Images" and "Feelings"

79. Leia   80. A   81. Leia and Luke's *real* mother   82. B   83. A
84. Leia   85. Wicket and Paploo   86. C   87. B   88. Completing
the boy's training and, in time, calling him "Master"   89. attack
90. A   91. Luke becoming his "servant"

Jedi Master Bonus #18: Admiral Piett

Jedi Master Bonus #19: apprentice

92. B   93. hatred   94. Vader   95. B   96. batteries

Jedi Master Bonus #20: Yoda

MAXIMUM SCORE POTENTIAL: 196
YOUR SCORE: _____

JEDI KNIGHTHOOD SCORING LEGEND

After you have totaled the points from each section to calculate your overall score, determine your level of training success and status as a Jedi Knight as follows:

2275–1926	**Jedi Master**
1925–1515	**Defender of the Galaxy (Full-Fledged Jedi Knight)**
1514–1179	**Guardian of Justice and Freedom (Jedi Knight-Errant)**
1178–850	**Just a Crazy Old Wizard**
849–534	**Cadet Candidate for Starfleet Academy**
533–201	**Sarlacc Snack**

Jedi Master

Congratulations! You are one of the few Jedi Knights powerful enough in the ways of the Force to have evolved into a Jedi Master, a status achieved only by our former mentor and teacher, the legendary Yoda. You now have moved beyond the need for weapons such as lightsabers, preferring instead to depend solely on the Force to give you the strength you desire. You are now one with your world, with the entire galaxy, bound to it through the ever-present and positive energy of the Force.

Defender of the Galaxy
[Full-Fledged Jedi Knight]

You have demonstrated your strength in the Force and thus have been awarded the rank of Jedi Knight, Defender of the Galaxy, and along with it all the rights, dignity and respected position the title holds. Although you now have a reputation for your supernatural skills with a lightsaber, your real power comes from your ability to tap into and manipulate the Force. Use it only for the protection and defense of the New Republic and *never, never* allow yourself to be seduced by the dark side.

Guardian of Justice and Freedom
[Jedi Knight-Errant]

You have successfully learned passivity over aggressiveness, understanding over assumption, and knowledge rather than force. Yet you cannot complete your training as a Jedi Knight because you lack patience and control. This is a dangerous time for you, when you will be tempted by the anger, fear, and aggression of the dark side of the Force. Mind what you have learned and do not choose the quick and easy path.

Just a Crazy Old Wizard

As a Force-sensitive being you have mastered most of the Jedi skills and techniques, except the ability to alter and change the distribution and nature of the Force to create illusions, move objects, and change the perceptions of others. Like any energy field, the Force can be manipulated, and knowledge of these manipulation techniques give the Jedi Knight his power. Until you learn to not be so reckless with your abilities, you will remain in training in the deserts of Tatooine, where the locals consider you "just a crazy old wizard."

Cadet Candidate for Starfleet Academy

Always with you it cannot be done. As Jedi Master Yoda would say, "Try not. Do. Or do not. There is no try." To be a Jedi you must have the deepest commitment, the most serious mind, either of which you are sorely lacking. You also yearn for adventure and excitement, but a Jedi Knight craves not these things. Your transfer credits have been forwarded to the registrar at Starfleet Academy where, hopefully, you can finish what you began. Face it, you're a washout.

Sarlacc Snack

Your true identity has been compromised! Bothan spies have provided us with detailed information that you are in reality a deep-cover intelligence agent for the Imperial Security Bureau (ISB). Because you failed in your covert mission to successfully infiltrate the New Republic through the Jedi Knights, we have learned through reliable sources that ISB officers intend to feed you to the terrible Sarlacc creature that lives in the desert wastes of Tatooine's Dune Sea, where you will die a slow, pain-filled death.

The Jedi Code:

"There is no emotion; there is peace.
There is no ignorance; there is knowledge.
There is no passion; there is serenity.
There is no death; there is the Force."

May the Force be with you . . . always!

BIBLIOGRAPHY

Altman, Mark. "The Wars You Never Saw." Sci-Fi Universe, July 1994.

Enrico, Dottie. "Dark Side of PepsiCo: Firm Links with 'Star Wars'." USA Today, May 16, 1996: 1B.

Fredrickson, Anthony. The World of Star Wars: A Compendium of Fact and Fantasy from Star Wars and the Empire Strikes Back. Paradise Press, Inc., Ridgefield, Connecticut, 1981.

Glut, Donald F. Star Wars: The Empire Strikes Back. Del Rey Books, New York, New York, 1980.

Gross, Edward. "Empire Builder." Cinescape, February 1996: 26–31.

Holly, Rob. "I, Robot." Cinescape, February 1996: 39.

Johnson, Joe and Nilo Nodis-Jamero. Star Wars: Return of the Jedi Sketchbook. Ballantine Books, New York, New York. 1983.

Kahn, James. Star Wars: Return of the Jedi. Del Rey Books, New York, New York, 1983.

Kaplan, David. "The Force Is Still With Him." Newsweek, May 13, 1996: 64.

Lane, Randall. "Master of Illusion." Reader's Digest, July 1996: 78–83.

Lucas, George. Star Wars: A New Hope. Del Rey Books, New York, New York, 1976.

McDonnell, David. Starlog's Science Fiction Heroes and Heroines. Crescent Books, New York, New York: 1995.

McQuarrie, Ralph. Star Wars: Return of the Jedi Portfolio. Ballantine Books, New York, New York: 1983.

McQuarrie, Ralph. The Star Wars Portfolio. Ballantine Books, New York, New York: 1977.

Nashawaty, Chris. "Back to the Future: Twenty Years Later, the Empire Strikes Back." Entertainment Weekly, August 2, 1996: 6–7.

Seiler, Andy. "The Real Box-Office Champs." USA Today, August 19, 1996: 1D-2D.

Slavicsek, Bill. Death Star Technical Companion. West End Games, Honesdale, Pennsylvania: 1991.

Slavicsek, Bill. A Guide to the Star Wars Universe (2nd Edition). Del Rey Books, New New York: 1984.

Slavicsek, Bill and Curtis Smith. Star Wars Sourcebook. West End Games, New York, New York: 1987.

Star Wars Insider Magazine, Issue #27.

Star Wars Insider Magazine, Issue #28.

Star Wars Insider Magazine, Issue #29.

Star Wars Insider Magazine, Issue #30.

Star Wars: Return of the Jedi Official Collectors Edition. Paradise Press, Inc., Newtown, Connecticut: 1983.

Star Wars: The Empire Strikes Back Notebook. Ballantine Books, New York, New York: 1980.

Star Wars: The Empire Strikes Back Official Collectors Edition. Paradise Press, Inc., Ridgefield, Connecticut: 1980.

Star Wars: The Movie Trilogy Sourcebook. West End Games, Honesdale, New York: 1993.

The Star Wars Album: Official Collectors Edition. Ballantine Books, New York, New York: 1977.

Vaz, Mark Cotta and Shinji Hata. From Star Wars to Indiana Jones: The Best of the Lucasfilm Archives. Chronicle Books, San Francisco, California: 1994.

Vebber, Dan. "Star Wars Lives." Sci-Fi Universe, November 1995: 28–31.

Velasco, Raymond L. A Guide to the Star Wars Universe. Del Rey Books, New York, New York: 1984.

About the Authors

James Hatfield is the former entertainment editor for *The Texas Women's News* and a frequent contributor to other Lone Star State regional publications. Having returned to his native Arkansas from Dallas in 1994, where he was for many years the vice-president of a large real estate management company, he now lives in a small town at the foothills of the Ozarks with his wife Nancy and their two previously homeless girls—Angel ("the Heinz 57 mutt") and Muffin ("the *very* independent Siamese feline"). James' other interests include hunting for antiques and fishing on Beaver Lake for "that trophy Bass."

George Burt, Ph.D. (affectionately known as "Doc") is a computer consultant to major businesses and industries in Texas, specializing in software application development. Doc met his co-author while working on a major computer project for one of America's largest retail companies. They have been writing partners ever since. Doc makes his home in Dallas, Texas, where he spends his leisure time reading law books (he's also a paralegal) or indulging in his real passion—cheering for the Super Bowl champion Dallas Cowboys!

Other Kensington Books by the Authors
The Ultimate Trek Trivia Challenge for the Next Generation
Patrick Stewart: The Unauthorized Biography
The Unauthorized X-Files Challenge